# The Will to Tell

## Memoirs of a Gombiner Survivor

Author: Yitzhak Weizman

**A Publication of JewishGen, INC**
**Edmond J. Safra Plaza, 36 Battery Place, New York, NY 10280**
**646.494.5972 | info@JewishGen.org | www.jewishgen.org**

**An affiliate of New York's Museum of Jewish Heritage – A Living
Memorial to the Holocaust**

## The Will to Tell

Copyright © 2022 Ilil, Henat and Menahem Weizman.
Published by JewishGen, Inc.
First printing: June 2022, Sivan 5782
Second Printing: August 2022, Av 5782

Author: Yitzhak Weizman
Translator: Dikla Yeffet-Weizman
Editor: Leon Zamosc
Cover Design: Jan R. Fine

Printed in the United States of America by Lightning Source, Inc.

Library of Congress Control Number (LCCN): 2022934182

ISBN: 978-1-954176-43-0 (hard cover: 150 pages, alk. paper)

**Credits and Captions for Book Cover:**

Front cover photograph: Yitzhak Weizman with parents and sister. Source: Yitzhak Weizman's family album.

Back cover photograph: Yitzhak Weizman giving testimony in 1997. Source: USC Shoah Foundation.

# About JewishGen.org

JewishGen, an affiliate of the Museum of Jewish Heritage - A Living Memorial to the Holocaust, serves as the global home for Jewish genealogy.

Featuring unparalleled access to 30+ million records, it offers unique search tools, along with opportunities for researchers to connect with others who share similar interests. Award winning resources such as the Family Finder, Discussion Groups, and ViewMate, are relied upon by thousands each day.

In addition, JewishGen's extensive informational, educational and historical offerings, such as the Jewish Communities Database, Yizkor Book translations, InfoFiles, Family Tree of the Jewish People, and KehilaLinks, provide critical insights, first-hand accounts, and context about Jewish communal and familial life throughout the world.

Offered as a free resource, JewishGen.org has facilitated thousands of family connections and success stories, and is currently engaged in an intensive expansion effort that will bring many more records, tools, and resources to its collections.

Please visit https://www.jewishgen.org/ to learn more.

**Executive Director:** Avraham Groll

*Yitzhak Weizman*

## About the JewishGen Press

JewishGen Press (formerly the Yizkor Books-in-Print Project) is the publishing division of JewishGen.org, and provides a venue for the publication of non-fiction books pertaining to Jewish genealogy, history, culture, and heritage.

In addition to the Yizkor Book category, publications in the Other Non-Fiction category include Shoah memoirs and research, genealogical research, collections of genealogical and historical materials, biographies, diaries and letters, studies of Jewish experience and cultural life in the past, academic theses, and other books of interest to the Jewish community.

Please visit https://www.jewishgen.org/Yizkor/ybip.html to learn more.

**Director of JewishGen Press:** Joel Alpert
**Managing Editor** - Jessica Feinstein
**Publications Manager** - Susan Rosin

# Foreword

### by Ilil, Henat and Hemy Weizman

The story of the life of our late father Yitzhak Weizman was only revealed to us, his three children, when we were already parents to our own children.

We always knew that he was a Holocaust survivor. He had the number 145227 tattooed on his arm.

But he told us very little about his Holocaust experiences. "It was a long time ago," he used to say, and "Polanyah" (as we called Poland at the time) seemed very far away. We studied in school and read books about it, but the Holocaust was not present in our home. Unlike other children of survivors, we were not pressured to eat everything on our plates and were even allowed to waste food. "It will not help the children of Africa if you eat everything," used to say our mother, who came from a family that had been living in Israel for six generations. Our father smiled.

What we did know was that our father's grandfather had been an important figure in his life. He was a successful industrialist and trader, one of the richest Jews in the town of Gombin. He introduced our father to the secrets of the family business, but he also wanted him to learn Judaism in the heder, the traditional school where Jewish boys received basic religious instruction. We also knew that our father participated on the youth movement Hashomer Hatzair, that he loved to play soccer, and that the horses in Gombin were fast – he used to say that the carts in Gombin, even when loaded with grain, were faster than the lazy soccer players in Israel.

We were aware that our father was the only survivor of his family. His father Menachem, his mother Hannah, and his sister Helcia had all been murdered during the Holocaust. But we did not really know how he had survived. He kept us ignorant about it. The shadows of the past remained outside the door.

Things changed when the grandchildren arrived. The new generation did not like to be kept ignorant about anything. They asked questions and wanted to receive answers. Our father could not resist them. Without the pressure of the grandchildren's questions, it is doubtful that this book would have ever been written.

We have read our father's story over and over again. He writes things as they were, almost like an objective bystander - avoiding hyperbole or emotional excess. With characteristic modesty, he writes: "I am not a hero and I never wanted to be a hero."

We emphasize this fact because the figure of speech "like cattle to the slaughter" burned our father's soul. In the times of the establishment of the State of Israel, that expression was often used to describe the way in which the Jews had perished during the Holocaust. When the country formally adopted the wording "Shoah veGvurah" (Holocaust and Heroism) to commemorate the tragedy, the relationship between the two concepts created difficult dilemmas for the construction of a new ethos in the Jewish state.

Our father's story is a story of coping. It is also a story about his disposition to discern points of light in the midst of darkness and preserve them in his mind.

As the readers will see in the book, the permanent effort to cope was our father's daily reality. We believe that some of the choices he made were truly heroic. One example is the story about his involvement in what he describes as an "interesting incident" in the Jędrzejów camp. Despite his lack of experience, he volunteered to replace the damaged wheel of a German officer's vehicle. In the process, he saved his life and that of his mates. Then, when he was given extra food as a reward for replacing the wheel, he chose to share it with his friends rather than keeping it for himself.

Our father's ability to recognize points of light is demonstrated by the story about the Auschwitz guard who caught him outside his barrack during roll call. The guard punished him with fifteen lashes, but then, to spare him from being caught and punished again by other guards, he accompanied him to his barrack. Our father writes: "I raised my face and we exchanged looks. He understood that I thanked him." Snared in the horrible reality of Auschwitz, our father, who was not a religious believer, was still able to recognize a glimmer of humanity as a source of hope for a different kind of life.

Although he did not try or want to be a hero, we see our father as such. He was a hero not only because he struggled to survive and showed courage in the face of unparalleled evil, but also because of his unwavering ability to preserve his humanity.

From his earliest youth, our father nurtured in his soul the ideal of Zionism. The description of his feelings when he first met Jewish Brigade soldiers from Eretz Israel conveys the depth of his identification with the State of Israel: "We could not believe our eyes. We were so proud of them! Just seeing them strengthened in me the wish to go to Eretz Israel. They awakened in me again all my latent dreams that suddenly became true. In my worst days of suffering, I had dreamt about seeing upright Jews, proud and carrying weapons."

Our father fought in Israel's wars and had the privilege of seeing the birth of the Jewish state. His humanity, the greatest preserved legacy of his life's travails, never left him, not did his ability to recognize the humanity and rights of others.

In one of his lectures to IDF soldiers, he was asked to single out his most difficult moment during the war. To the soldiers' astonishment, he replied: "The moment of liberation." Pressed to explain, he added: "It was then that I really realized that I was alone in the world."

Dear father, you have not been and will never be alone.

We love you and miss you,

Your children Ilil, Henat and Hemy (Menahem).

Your grandchildren Danny, Miki (Michael), Shai, Noam, Tom, Sefi (Yosef), Rotem and Amir.

And all your great-grandchildren.

March 2022

*Yitzhak Weizman*

# Translator's Note

I am not a professional translator and English is not my first language, so I am sure that this translation is far from perfect. Still, it faithfully reflects the facts as remembered by my husband Yitzhak and I hope that I was able to capture the feelings and emotions that he expressed in his memoir.

I am grateful to my young neighbor and friend Erga Cohen, a South African University graduate, for reading the translation and correcting my mistakes.

Dikla Yeffet-Weizman

August 2003

# Editor's Note

Yitzhak Weizman was born in Gombin, Poland on July 13, 1928 and passed away in Rishon LeZion, Israel on August 5, 2015. He wrote his memoirs at the age of sixty-six and deposited the typescript in the archives of Yad Vashem in Jerusalem. In 2003, his wife Dikla Yeffet-Weizman translated the original text and two additional postscripts into English.

As editor of the translation, I corrected spelling and grammatical errors and adjusted the choice of words to the overall tone of the book. Occasionally, I consulted the original Hebrew text and modified the structure of paragraphs to make sure that the ideas were clearly conveyed. None of these changes affected the factual content of the information, which was preserved as provided by the author.

The original Hebrew typescript did not include images. The photographs featured in this book come from the author's family album and from various archival collections. Their provenance is distinguished by the captions, which describe the family pictures with wording from the author's text, and reference the archival images with explanatory lines and source citations.

Yitzhak Weizman's memoirs are organized sequentially, with separate chapters recounting his experiences in the different places where he was during and after the war. Writing fifty years after the events, his timing references were usually vague, and he was unable to recall the names of the last two camps where he worked in Germany during the final months of the war. Cross-referencing the details of his recollections with other sources (published materials, archival documents including prisoner cards, and diaries and testimonies of other survivors), I was able to ascertain the dates of some of his displacements, identify the two unnamed camps in Germany, and clarify a confusion related to his sailing from Italy to Mandatory Palestine. I have included the most relevant information from my supplementary research in a few footnotes inserted at appropriate points of the narrative.

Leon Zamosc

March 2022

**A map of Yitzhak Weizman's displacements as forced laborer, refugee, and illegal immigrant between March 1942 and January 1947.**

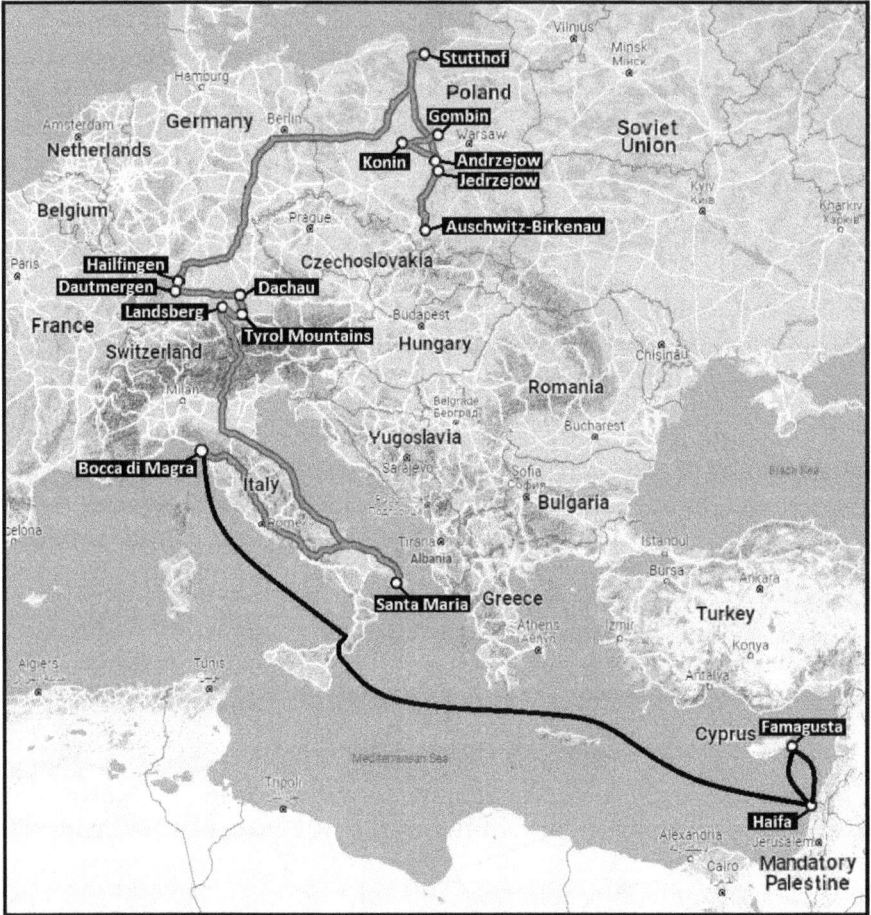

# Contents

# Author's Preface

Since the end of the Second World War many written testimonies of victims and survivors of the Nazi Holocaust have been published. Behind each one of these testimonies is the tortured soul of a human being who mustered the will to tell - to tell the world, the Jews, the next generations, and all those who were not directly touched by the Nazi cataclysm. Very few of the people who experienced the despair, agonies, and atrocities have survived. In one way or another, they are all physically and mentally scarred.

Some may think that, on the basis of the available information and their own judgment, they can come to terms with the whole truth about the Holocaust and perhaps understand and suggest solutions to the riddle of human motives. But it is doubtful that they will ever be really able to comprehend the magnitude of what happened to the Jews during the Second World War.

I have no doubt that, like me, most survivors worry that the passage of time will blur the memory of the Holocaust and its implications. But we must understand that it is not too late, that the Holocaust is not simply an obsession of the survivors, and that its consequences are not only relevant for those who personally experienced them. The Holocaust is part of the collective memory of all the Jews, wherever they are. That is why, despite the fact that many years have passed, I feel the inner need to tell, to the best of my humble ability, what I went through during the war.

For a long time I repressed the memories. I did not share them with those who were close to me, not even with my children. I felt guilty because I could not make sense of the fact that I was the only survivor from my family. I also worried about causing psychological trauma to my children, fearing that they would not be able to cope with the truth about deeds of such cruelty. Besides, Israeli society was not yet ready to acknowledge that we did not go "like cattle to the slaughter." People were not prepared to recognize that the daily struggle for survival in inhuman conditions had been a form of heroism of the first order. It was painful for the survivors to face that lack of empathy, especially on the part of old-timers who had arrived before the war and had participated in the Jewish self-defense organizations in the times of the British Mandate. Thankfully, the atmosphere has changed over the years, and it is easier now to open up and tell the story to the younger generations.

Thus, at the age of sixty-six, forty years after the end of the Second World War, I am revisiting here all the events and experiences that I went through during the war. I am writing for the memory of the family that I lost in the Holocaust and for the new family that I raised in Israel.

# PART I

# My family and home

I was born on July 13, 1928 in Gombin, a small town in central Poland near the city of Płock. Gombin, which is spelled "Gąbin" in Polish, was the town of my paternal family. My father was Menahem Mendel Weizman and my mother's maiden name was Hanna Kerber. My sister Helcia was one year older than me. About half of the residents of Gombin were Jews, most of them craftsmen and small merchants. My maternal family was considered one of the wealthiest in the district. My mother's father, Leibl Kerber, owned a leather-processing factory that was technologically advanced for those times. Several hundred employees worked in the factory, which occupied an entire street with dozens of buildings, warehouses and yards.

The factory included yards with fruit orchards and a processing plant for dried fruit, jam and marmalade. Through the orchards ran a small, deep river where we loved to swim in the summer and skate during the winter. In addition to the tannery, my mother's family traded in furs. My father had a small glue factory that was located in an open field outside the town because of the unpleasant smells released by the production process.

My memories as a child are of a close family that convened often for discussions, accounting and decision-making. I understood parts of what was said. From a young age I was aware of what was going on around me, especially because my grandfather and my father asked me to sit at the table where the discussions were held in the evening. They saw me as the intended heir and they wanted me to know the trade secrets. I learned how to think carefully, quickly if needed, which helped me later when I faced the horrors of the war as a young lonely boy.

In our immediate family we were two children – my sister and me. My mother married my father relatively late because it was her second marriage (I learned about it only later in Israel from a distant relative). Her first husband had died shortly after their wedding, before they could have any children. When I heard the story I understood why my mother was always so anxious, keeping us close, and spoiling and hugging us in a way that was somewhat exaggerated. On one occasion, I was supposed to go on a school trip by boat up the Vistula river to Warsaw. My mother refused to let me go, out of fear that something could happen to me. I was disappointed because I had planned to meet a girl from Warsaw with whom I had been corresponding for a long time (it had started as a pen-pal project encouraged by a teacher). I learned from that experience that over-caring is not a virtue. One must always find the right balance to overcome fright and anxiety.

Our small family lived separately from the extended family, in a largely Christian neighborhood of the western part of Gombin. I spent a lot of my childhood time at my grandfather's place in the Jewish neighborhood. There, I met in the yard with my classmates, playing and thinking of ways to deal with the Polish boys that harassed us on our way to school.

They beat us, set their dogs on us and shouted: "Jews – go to Palestine, your place is not here, you killed Jesus our Lord." As children we did not understand why they hated us - we were sure that we had not caused harm to anyone. That hostility made us think. From a tender age we wondered who we were, how we were different from the others, and what had we done to deserve their hate.

I began to find answers to those questions when I joined the youth movement Hashomer Hatzair, which was very active in our town. Many of my friends were members and the leaders were wonderful guides. Most of those guides went to Eretz Israel (then called Palestine) before the war and founded or joined kibbutzim, including Evron, Ein Hachoresh, Negba, Eilon, Galon and others. Some of them are still alive.

As a member of Hashomer Hatzair, I soon understood that the best solution to our predicament in Poland was going to Eretz Israel. It was a dream that perhaps some day would be fulfilled – who could know?

My mother's sister Rachel lived in Zychlin, a town near Gombin. Her husband Yaakov Bol was a wholesale merchant who dealt in construction materials. The fact that his business was located on a railroad junction enabled him to trade all over Poland. They had two children – a boy and a girl called Shlamek and Fela who were older than me. In 1938 they moved to Łódź, a big city where my uncle opened a textile business. I visited them often as a boy and I remember that they were quite well to do.

With my parents, Hanna and Menahem Mendel Weizman, and my sister Helcia.

My mother Hanna née Kerber.

Gombin school. I am sitting second from left. The third teacher from left is my cousin Sala Magnes.

One of the groups of the Zionist youth movement Hashomer Hatzair in Gombin.

My father (sitting first from right) with his friends from the Bund.

On my father's side the family was larger – one sister and five brothers. It was a poor family. My grandfather Meyer and his wife Simcha had a small grocery store and it had been difficult for them to raise and educate their children. They were simple, good-natured people who received me warmly when I visited them during school vacations. I have fond memories of them.

Visiting the city of Płock in the years before the war I met cousins from my father's side of the family. They were the children of my uncles Shlomo and Tzvi. My father had three other siblings who had already left Poland. His sister Anna and his brother Moshe Aharon were living in France and his brother Leon had emigrated to Chile.

I had a pleasant life and the best of everything until the outbreak of the Second World War in September 1939.

# The beginning of the war

Poland was conquered quickly - it only took a few weeks. Many Jews fled to the lands that were under Soviet rule on the other side of the river Bug. Near our town, the Polish army offered strong resistance. For that reason, Gombin was heavily bombed. Many people were killed or wounded.

During the raids the four of us hugged each other – my parents, my sister, and me. We would stay alive or die together. We sought shelter in a wooden house that had two cellars - both of them were full to capacity. We were fortunate that our cellar was spared by the bombs. The other one received a direct hit that killed or wounded most of the people.

After that terrifying experience, we decided that we would rush to an open field or to the woods, so that we could watch the maneuvers of the airplanes and run accordingly. The bombings went on incessantly for two days.

Finally, the Polish army broke down and started to withdraw. We saw long caravans of tired soldiers retreating. Many of them demanded civilian clothes to replace their uniforms and avoid capture by the Germans. They vented their frustration cursing and beating the Jews. They found a culprit – the Jew.

From the moment the Germans occupied the town things changed drastically. The center of Gombin had been mostly destroyed. Somehow, my grandfather's house had not been hit, so all of us stayed with him. I do not mention my maternal grandmother because she died at the age of fifty-four and my memories of her are vague. My grandfather married again, but I did not have much of a relationship with his second wife.

Life became very hard. There was no regular supply of food to the town and the Jewish population was deliberately prevented from trying to get it. The Jewish children were not allowed to go to school.

We were ordered to wear patches with a yellow Star of David and could not leave the town or send letters. We were cut off from the rest of our family and the world. It was forbidden under death penalty to have or listen to a radio (radios were still rare in those times - we did

The synagogue of Gombin. Image source: Gombin Society.

Market day in Gombin. Image source: Gombin Society.

German occupation of Gombin. Image source: Towarzystwo Miłośników Ziemi Gąbińskiej.

Entrance to the Gombin ghetto. Image source: Gombin Society.

Forced Jewish workers in Gombin. Image source: Gombin Society.

Gombin Firemen's Hall. Image source: Towarzystwo Miłośników Ziemi Gąbińskiej.

not have one). The Germans confiscated Jewish property – houses, shops and factories. All trade was stopped. Our factory, warehouses and merchandise were immediately seized.

Fortunately for us, the Germans entrusted the management of the factory to a man who had trade relations with our family before the war. His name was Schneider, from a Polish family of German origin. The Germans called them "Volksdeutsches." The humane way in which he treated us was praiseworthy. He brought us food supplies to the best of his ability. For us it was lifesaving. For him it was a risk that took great courage. If he was caught he could lose his job and be severely punished. Later on, he was appointed as mayor of Gombin by the Germans and we lost contact with him.

My grandfather and my father decided to hide all the valuables that they had in the house. I helped my father open a hole in the concrete floor of one of the warehouses in my grandfather's yard. We hid three brass kettles with glass jars full of gold, diamonds and American dollars. If that warehouse was not later demolished and excavated for a new building, the kettles may still be there. We hid valuables in every possible place. My father filled the hollow curtain rods with foreign currency and we carried gold and diamonds in seam pockets sewn into our clothes. It was heavy but there was no alternative. We were tense all the time. Any minute there could be an order about a search, deportation, or transport to a forced labor camp far from Gombin.

About a year after the occupation, the Germans concentrated the Jews in a designated area of the town. We moved to an apartment that we had to share with other families. It was terribly overcrowded and there was no privacy at all. The streets where the Jews lived were fenced and watched by armed guards. No entrance and no exit. We were in the Gombin ghetto.

A daily struggle for survival started. Whole families stood in long queues in the rain and cold to get a loaf of bread, with ration cards according to family size. In that situation, all thoughts and energies focused on how to get food and with whom to associate in order to survive.

The Germans imposed a system of forced labor on the Jews. In disgraceful conditions and under strict vigilance, groups of Jews were taken to work outside the ghetto. When passing the gate on their way to work, they received a daily ration of food. My father managed to get a job in the leather factory that had belonged to us. He saved his food ration and we shared it in the evening. He had to work hard and I am sure that he was hungry all through the day, but he overcame it for the sake of all of us. Only those who have known real hunger can understand the strength of mind that is required for that.

My grandfather Leibl was too old to get a job and too young to be included in the list of workers. But he was very resourceful and found ways to adapt to the situation. He established roundabout relations with non-Jewish acquaintances from before the war and was able to occasionally buy food for the family. Thanks to that, we endured. It was a meager, bare existence, but we were doing better than others who soon began to show signs of deterioration because of the lack of food.

In 1941 my grandfather fell seriously ill. He was bedridden with a badly infected leg. His suffering was terrible and there were no medications. We did our best to help him but it was to no avail. After several weeks of horrible pain he passed away. My mother, who had just broken her leg, could not go to the funeral. I remember how heartbroken she was about that.

My grandfather had the money and the connections. With his death, our family lost its dominant figure. We felt orphaned. There was a deep sense of insecurity and helplessness.

My father took charge. He had been an active member of the Gombin branch of the Bund party before the war and was able to build a network of contacts with people outside the ghetto. He had connections with Jews who were hiding in the Arian side and activists of the Polish Socialist Party who had gone underground under the Nazi occupation. Through secret contacts and in dangerous ways my father managed to get food for the family, even more than my grandfather. It was quite an achievement considering the difficult conditions of humiliation, suffering and hunger.

In the ghetto there was a Jewish committee – the Judenrat. The committee had been established by the Germans and its members were forced to fulfill every order received from them.

As time went by, the Jewish population was physically weakened. The number of sick people grew. The Judenrat was ordered to prepare a list of old, sick and disabled people for transportation. The ghetto was in turmoil. People rushed around pleading, arguing and

11

lobbying. By the deadline, the list was not ready. The Germans gave an ultimatum to the Judenrat – if they failed to submit the list within the next twenty-four hours, they would be the first deportees.

The list was submitted. I want to believe that the Judenrat did not know that the transport was intended for extermination. The Germans said that the deportees would be taken to hospitals and sanatoriums. Not one of them ever returned to Gombin.

In 1941, two years after I had stopped going to school, I volunteered as an apprentice in a smithy located near the ghetto. A local "Volksdeutsche" ran the workshop for the Germans. Despite of my mother's objections, I worked from dawn until late at night. Although I was not paid or given benefits, I liked to work. Learning a trade was good for me, and there was another reason for my dedication to the job – escaping from the trouble and pain of the family at home. I quickly progressed, became part of the team, and started getting rations like a regular worker. For the first time I became a factor in my family, contributing my share to the struggle for survival. My parents were proud and praised me. My work gave me a feeling of independence and self-security. I began to believe that I could deal with the situation despite all the difficulties.

It was the beginning of 1942. We, especially me, had no clue of what was going on in the war and in the world at large. There was no information source. But we had adapted to a life of poverty and hunger and we were still together as a family, taking care of each other.

# Partings

In the winter of 1942 my father was among the men who were ordered to report to the Firemen's Hall of Gombin, which was in the town center outside the ghetto. There was great grief at home. My mother and sister cried terribly and we all felt powerless. I tried to get help through my work connections but nothing worked. My father and the other men were taken away to a forced labor camp in Germany (I cannot remember its name). We received two postcards from him, which was rare because the Germans did not allow correspondence. We sent him packages with clothes, but I doubt that he ever received them.

I learned about my father's fate later on, when I was in Birkenau, Auschwitz. I met other Gombiner Jews who came from the camps in Germany. They told me that my father had died in the labor camp as a result of severe illness. But they offered no details. They only said that he had suffered terribly. I could not accept the story. My father was a strong, healthy man and he had only been in the camp for a few months. I doubted that he could have deteriorated so much in such a short time. I persisted with my questions until they finally told me that he had died from beatings and torture. My father could not accept the conditions in the camp. He was one of the rebels and it cost him his life.

My father had strong political ideas. He was prepared to fight and pay a price if need be. I heard that in the mid-1930s he had thought about volunteering to fight in the Spanish civil war but my mother did not allow him to do it. He always voiced his opinions. As an activist of the Bund, he was a socialist Jew who engaged in fiery debates with people who held different views. He sacrificed his life as someone who resisted in the German camps. The Gombiners who were with him said that if he had been less of a radical, and more careful about voicing his opinions, he would have had a better chance to survive.

The fact that he had married the daughter of a wealthy man had not changed my father's political views. He had grown up in a poor home full of children and had started supporting himself quite young. I can definitely understand the choice that he made in the last days of his life.

When my father was taken from home I was almost fourteen years old. We remained the three of us: my mother, my sister and me. I felt the need to prove that I could take care of the family. I put more effort in my job, toiling day and night in order to meet the needs of our basic existence.

In the ghetto, the Germans degraded us to a mental state in which all our senses and thoughts were absorbed by one thing: getting food to lessen our hunger. All the other activities of normal civilized people vanished from our life. That was how they succeeded in neutralizing our will to resist.

The only means I had at my disposal were my drive to survive and my ability to work. My mother told me: "You had to become a man before your time." I was happy and proud to hear that.

But that situation did not last. On March 8, 1942, the Judenrat was ordered to submit a list of all the men aged fifteen to fifty. Since I was not yet fifteen, I was not included. That night, while we were in bed, a group of "Volksdeutsches" and soldiers raided our place, overturning everything and beating us. They demanded to know where my father was and whether there were other able-bodied men in the house. My mother said that my father had been drafted for work in Germany, showing his postcards as proof. She said that I was under the age of fifteen, but the explanations were of no use. They kept shouting, breaking things and hitting us with the butts of their guns.

My mother grabbed me with one hand and held my sister with the other. They fought, begged and cried to prevent the Germans from taking me away. They were beaten until they fainted and lied on the floor. I was also beaten and dragged out of the house. The Germans had decided that I was fit enough for work in the camps.

I will never forget that tragic moment – how I hugged my mother and sister, their heart breaking cries, and their pleading to go with me. On that moment, I was taken from them forever.

14

# **All alone**

In the street, the Germans pushed me towards a large group of Jews surrounded by armed guards. We were taken to the Firemen's Hall in the town's center. The place was packed with hundreds of nervous men. I met relatives, classmates, and acquaintances. One of my friends told me: "I have just seen Meyer Laski, he is here with a German officer conducting a search." Meyer Laski had owned the smithy where I worked in the ghetto and he was a member of the Judenrat. "You should go and talk with him, he knows you, maybe he can get you released."

I tried to call Meyer Laski's attention but he ignored me. That hurt me dreadfully. Throughout my years in the labor camps, I felt that I would never forgive him. After surviving the war, however, I found myself thinking that I should be grateful to him for not preventing my deportation to the labor camps. Going to the camps spared me from extermination with all those who stayed behind in Gombin's ghetto, including my mother and sister.

For a whole day we stayed in the Firemen's Hall without food or water. The Germans worked on the list. Fortunately, they accepted my oral statement that I was over the age of fifteen. I thought that it was better to go to work than staying in Gombin with the old and sick people.

After long hours of overcrowding and noise, an SS man in black uniform with a swastika on his sleeve stepped on the podium and shouted: "Quiet! Sit on the floor in horizontal lines, so that we can count how many people are in the hall!" Since the order was not fulfilled as quickly as he wanted, he fired his gun in the air and shouted: "If in two minutes you are not properly seated I will shoot anyone who is out of line."

Minutes later there was another shot. The bullet whizzed near me and hit my mother's uncle Hershl Kerber (brother of my grandfather Leibl Kerber). He fell bleeding on me. He had been hit in the head. I shivered all over, covered with his blood.

I was ordered, together with three other men, to take him out and let him die in one of the corridors. Not far from him, his two sons witnessed his murder. They were helpless. Nobody was allowed to utter a sound. Not to shout and not to cry.

That was my first meeting with the SS.

On the next day they gave us a cup of what was supposed to be soup and loaded us on a truck – standing, crowded like cattle. We left under heavy guard to an unknown place. As we passed through the town some Polish residents expressed their joy. They clapped, laughed, and made cut-throat gestures with their hands. We were trapped between two enemies that hated us blindly.

# The camp in Konin[1]

After a long drive we reached the labor camp in Konin, a town in the district of Poznan. Most of the Gombiners who were sent to forced labor during the war were first brought to that camp. The camp was outside the town, on open land without unwanted neighbors or observers.

The camp was fenced and the wretched shacks where we were going to sleep had leaks. Each one of us got an army blanket and a place on a wooden plank with some straw. The planks were arranged on top of each other. To get to "bed" we had to climb and crawl inside. The gap between the planks was so small that we could only lie down. It was impossible to sit.

Since we did not see other Jews, we thought that we were the first prisoners in the camp. From the moment we arrived, everything was dictated by the Germans' orders, according to a schedule that we had to fulfill under strict vigilance. They gave us one hour to clean the shacks and took us to the camp's square for roll call. The camp commander spelled out the rules and procedures. After that, each one of us was assigned a prisoner number. We became numbers without names or identities. Later on, we got a cup inscribed with our number and stood in a long line to get our "soup" - just warm water without taste or smell. It would have to be enough until next morning. The hunger did not allow us to fall asleep and we started feeling faint. At dawn, when we went out to work, we got our daily ration of bread: a fifth of a loaf. We were supposed to receive a

---

[1] Editor's note] The camp was located in Czarkow, near Konin's train station. The main source about the fate of its prisoners is Rabbi Yehoshua Moshe Aaronson's book *Alei Merorot [Leaves of Bitterness]*, posthumously published in Bnei Brak, Israel, in 1996. Aaronson was the rabbi of Sanniki (a tiny shtetl near Gombin) and his book includes the diary that he secretly kept in the Konin camp. The diary confirms that Yitzhak Weizman spent almost a year in the camp, arriving on March 9 1942 with a group of 861 deportees from Sanniki, Gombin and Gostynin, and leaving on February 24, 1943 with a transport of 129 inmates sent to the Andrzejów camp near Łódź (*Alei Merorot*, pp. 94-95 and 121-122). The list of the men transferred to Andrzejów (which includes Yitzhak Weizman's name) was not published in Aaronson's book, but it was given by his son to Ada Holtzman, who posted it online in 1998 (http://www.zchor.org/ALEI.HTM).

quarter, but the men who cut the loaves and distributed the rations stole some of the bread.

That night we heard a lot of noise. The camp was suddenly full of people. We realized that there were other Jews in the camp. They were now returning from their day of work. Among them I found acquaintances, including Avraham Najdorf, an older man who had once been a business partner of our family. He used to live in Płock, but he had joined his son and his son-in-law in Gombin when the war started. The three of them had been among the first taken to Konin and by now they were among the prisoners' representatives, who had some influence on things like work schedule and food distribution. I was lucky because, from time to time, they managed to give me more soup and sometimes more bread. Those occasional additions helped me overcome the initial crisis until my body adapted.

The work was physically very hard, from dawn until nightfall. We worked for Hochtief, a German company that used slave labor in projects of railway construction. Each work group included ten men under the watch of two soldiers with dogs. There were no breaks and we were not allowed to talk. We could only relieve ourselves by special permission, always accompanied by a guard.

I will never forget my first day of work. We had to unload wood logs and carry them to the place where they were laid on the ground for the railway tracks. Two men carried each log. I was paired with a very tall man, which unloaded most of the weight on me. When I suggested that I should have a different partner I was flogged on the spot for seeking "privileges." As additional punishment, they denied me the bread ration on the following morning. I learned my lesson – there was no choice but submitting to the rules.

Later on, my relations with the guards improved. They recognized that I was a useful worker. At one point, we dared to ask permission to go to a nearby village and get food from the Polish farmers. The guards agreed that one member of the group could go, but on one condition – if he did not return, the rest of the group would be shot. It was a decent gesture of the guards. They put themselves at risk because, if discovered, they could be punished. There were very few cases like that - it was an exception. In any case, the food that we occasionally managed to get in the village enabled us to hold on. In return for the gesture, we did our best to increase our productivity. Our guards boasted that they had the best group.

Every evening on our way back to the camp we passed by a small railway station. We always saw empty wagons that were parked on the side while the tracks were shifted. One evening we reached the station and, what did we see? Wagons full of carrots, potatoes and other vegetables! We climbed on them like crazy and started filling our pockets. The vegetables were worth more than gold for us. The guards yelled, fired in the air, and ordered us to return the stuff. When we refused to surrender our treasure, the guards gave up and led us to the camp.

At the gate, however, they had a surprise for us. They forced us to take off our clothes, cast the vegetables aside, and report naked to the gate guards. There we stood in the snow and cold, holding our garments in our hands. After an inspection accompanied by yelling and beatings, we had to run naked to the shack. By the door stood several SS men who flogged us viciously. Those who whined were lashed some more.

We entered the shacks in pain, exhausted and frozen. That evening there was no hot "soup" for us. We went to sleep hungry and frightened, but the Germans were not satisfied yet. After midnight, the camp commander broke into the shacks with guards and dogs. They took us out, half naked and without shoes, to stand in the snow for roll call under a temperature of minus twenty degrees Celsius. The commander shouted that anyone who moved would be executed and we were kept standing for a whole hour. Some men collapsed and were shot on the spot. Others had their feet frozen so badly that they could no longer use the wooden clogs that were our footwear. They had to strap up their feet and legs with rags and try to go on functioning.

I had horrible frostbites. The skin of my feet peeled off completely, and my big left toe was frozen and paralyzed – it stayed numb for a long time. Compared to the others, my injuries were slight because I had managed to stand on a bare stone and not on the ice and snow.

Our "sin" had long-term consequences. They changed our guards, we were watched more closely, and our working conditions worsened. After several weeks there were visible effects among the men. People who had once been fat and loved to eat were the first to break down.

Some of them became insane and committed suicide by cutting their veins or hanging themselves. Others collapsed from exhaustion.

I had never been a big eater, and the fact that my body had learned to adapt allowed me to keep going under the new conditions. I lost a lot of weight and got much weaker, but not to the point of near death. I was lucky that I was not among those who were deported because they were unable to continue working. Every several weeks there was a selection. The sick and weak were dispatched to a secret destination. It was only later that we learned where they were taken and what happened to them.

The year 1942 was coming to its end. That winter was particularly hard. There was no heating in the shacks and the cold was extreme. We had nothing to cover ourselves and could not fall asleep. The chill forced us to go to the toilet several times each night, but the latrines were far away. It was excruciating. We began to feel apathetic, no longer caring about our surroundings or what was going on in the distant world. We had no connection with any source of information. We were losing the sense of humanity. The only thing that remained was our survival instinct – the feeling of hunger and the urge to hold on.

They kept taking us out to work, even on the days of heavy snow, sometimes pointlessly because the accumulation of snow prevented the fulfillment of any tasks. But the German masters had to follow procedure. We had to go out even if we stood idle. The main point was to humiliate us, to trample our dignity to the point of complete prostration. It was a deliberate system of degradation and it succeeded.

In the first weeks of 1943 there were rumors that the camp would be closed. The representatives of the Jewish prisoners were ordered to submit a list of all the men who were unable to work. The representatives, which included the already mentioned Najdorf family, knew very well what the fate of the deported was going to be. This time, they refused to cooperate, even under the threat that they would be deported themselves. That evening we were ordered to come out of the shacks for roll call. The commander of the camp was enraged. He could not understand how they dared disobey him. He gave them an ultimatum. If by the next day the list was not submitted, the representatives would be hanged in the camp's square. It was a matter of German policy that the ugly job of preparing the list had to be done by the Jews. For the "master nation," it was not enough to conceive the idea of extermination – they had to further debase the Jews, forcing them to do the dirty work of selection.

The representatives asked to be excused from work in order to prepare the list. The commander of the camp agreed. On the following day, while everyone was at work, the representatives set the camp on fire with kerosene stolen from the kitchen. While the buildings were burning down, they committed suicide hanging themselves, including Avraham Najdorf and his son-in-law Fajwisz Kamlarz. It was a deed of extreme courage - an open act of refusal to forced cooperation with the Germans. We saw them as heroes who deserved our full esteem and admiration.

After the destruction of the camp, we had no roof over our heads. The Germans conducted a selection and deported a large group of men. Only a few of us stayed working in the camp. Since the shacks were not rebuilt, we had to sleep in the open. After several days, they transferred us to another forced labor camp near the city of Łódź.

New arrivals in a yard of the Konin labor camp. Around each man's neck is a paper tag with his personal details. Image source: Ghetto Fighters House Archives.

Konin Catholic Cemetery. Mass grave of Jewish victims of the Konin camp. Image Source: Muzeum Okręgowe w Koninie.

Monument commemorating the forced workers who perished in the construction of the Łódź-Olechów railway junction during the German occupation. Between 1940 and 1944, the project took the lives of thousands of Jewish slave laborers from Łódź ghetto and the Andrzejów and Jędrzejów forced labor camps. Image source: Muzeum Miasta Łodzi.

# Andrzejów[2]

Only half a year had passed since I had been torn from the arms of my mother and sister. Physically and mentally I had changed completely. I was obsessed by one thought – how to overcome the constant torture of hunger. The suffering was so atrocious that I could not think about anything else.

We were bound by the "contract" imposed to us by the Germans: if someone tried to escape, the whole group would be executed. My thinking and will to resist were conditioned by that. The bitter truth was that, even if it occurred to me to run away, there was nowhere to go. The Poles were anti-Semitic and they were also frightened. There was no way that they would hide and feed an unknown Jew. They knew that, if caught, they would be executed. Some of them informed the Germans about other Poles who were hiding Jews. They did it out of fear. That was also a result of the German policy – if a Jew was found in hiding, the whole village was punished.

There was no choice. We were trapped without any way out. Staying in the camp with a work group was the only alternative. I also had to consider my appearance. I looked typically Jewish. No one would take the risk of hiding or employing me.

There were few of us left, about one hundred men. The labor camp to which we were transferred was outside the small town Andrzejów, not far from Łódź. We went on working for the same Hochtief company, doing the same work. The camp was adjacent to a larger camp for English prisoners of war. Only a fence separated us from them.

Compared to Konin, our conditions were better. For one thing, we could talk with the English prisoners across the fence. After a long time of isolation, we finally had access to some information about what was going on in the front and in the world. The English

---

[2] [Editor's note] The prisoners of the forced labor camps of Andrzejów and Jędrzejów (next chapter) worked in the construction of the Łódź-Olechów railway junction. The supplementary sources indicate that Yitzhak Weizman spent the Spring and Summer of 1943 in these two camps. He arrived in Andrzejów from Konin on February 24 (note 1, page 17), was transferred from Andrzejów to Jędrzejów three-four months later, and arrived in Auschwitz from Jędrzejów on September 2 (note 3, page 34).

prisoners did not work and were treated in accordance with the Geneva Convention.

Our work conditions and food rations were the same as in Konin, but there were a couple of important differences. In Andrzejów, the guards were "Volksdeutsches." They were less strict than the Germans and sometimes more considerate. They occasionally brought us food and even clothes. On the other hand, we had conversations with civilian workers who came from Germany to work for the company. Most of them said that they opposed the Nazi régime. They also helped us with food. It was all very hush-hush, but they encouraged us to hang on. They said that the Germans would be defeated on the Russian front and that the Russians would counterattack. I did not fully understand their strategic analysis but they gave me faith and hope.

In Andrzejów, I had another opportunity to work in a smithy. Once again I proved to be an excellent worker. My craftsmanship was highly appreciated. I was still less than fifteen years old, but I had the skills that I had acquired in Gombin. The manager of the smithy was a German civilian who treated me with respect and appreciation. He gave me enough food so that I would not be hungry. I was even able to share food with my work mates.

I worked very hard. I often spent the whole day in the smithy, handling a five-kilogram hammer along with German craftsmen who were strong, healthy and skilled. I had no choice. I had to keep up with their work pace if I wanted to be a member of the team. It required an enormous physical effort.

The men who were not in the workshops had to work in the field, suffering hunger and humiliations. They had no contact with anyone except the guards, who were also supervised and had to make sure that the daily quotas of work were fulfilled. It was impossible for the workers to get any help.

We were constantly struggling to keep going and avoid reaching the stage of complete exhaustion, which was the Germans' goal. The guards spurred us saying that the Third Reich would not feed people who did not contribute to the war effort. The German machine performed with uncanny accuracy. They knew the limits of a person's endurance under those extreme conditions. The periodic transports punctually left the camp, taking away the weak and sick according to the German schedule.

I did very well in my job. I became the assistant operator of a bulldozer and was responsible for its daily maintenance. The German manager used to tell the other prisoners that "Ignatz (my name in Polish) should be your model. He is not a merchant or a thief. He is a respectable artisan who knows how to work. Follow his example and you will be better off." I understood very well that I had the means for survival. I got a reputation among the civilian workers, who wanted to have me as their assistant. That was how I ended up working for the chief manager, who was one of the oldest German civilians employed by the company. He was responsible for me and I went with him to all kinds of places without any special vigilance. He always reminded me that his life depended on me. If I ran away, ten people would be executed, including him. Again, I was bound by the same "contract." I could not betray the old man and my work mates.

I wanted to believe in people. The way I was treated by the civilian workers gave me hope that the Germans still had a glimmer of humanity. I had long chats with one of them. His name was Hans Schmidt. He was one of the youngest civilians and he had leftist, anti-Nazi beliefs. It was not clear why he was not in the army. He worked for the company as a locksmith. He was very courageous, openly voicing his opinions. People like him were in danger of ending up in some concentration camp as political prisoners.

Hans encouraged me to hold on. He said that "after the crushing defeat of the damned Nazis" we should keep in touch. It was only the beginning of 1943, but he thought that the Germans had already lost the war and that the real question was how long it would take them to surrender. They faced resistance in all the occupied territories. It was harder to send men and supplies to the front because the partisans sabotaged the railways, which the Germans were trying to repair with starved slaves who were not able to work. He often told me: "I know the truth. Hang on, do not give up. We shall meet after the war as free men and have a glass of beer together."

Those words still resonate in my ears. At first, I did not believe him. I thought that he wanted to set me up and I kept my mouth shut. He would say: "I understand your silence. It is obvious what you think about the Nazis. Their megalomania has driven them crazy." In the end, Hans' words affected me. I trusted him because I felt that he was honest, wise and reliable. He believed in the workers' rights and gave me hope. Hans was an exceptional case. I appreciated him even more when I later met the German political prisoners in

Auschwitz. Their fate was not different from that of the Jews. To my regret I did not meet Hans after the war.

# Jędrzejów

We were in Andrzejów for three or four months. Then we were transferred to another camp in neighboring Jędrzejów, where we continued to work for the same company.

Before the transfer there was a selection and the sick and weak were sent to the secret destination. None of them survived. That transport included two classmates with whom I had grown up in Gombin. Of my friends from primary school, only one remained. His name was Lajzer Bocian. He also survived the war, but he did not go to Eretz-Israel - he went to one of his uncles in America.

There were few other Gombiners in Jędrzejów. In general, our situation changed for the worse. In Andrzejów we had contacts with the English prisoners of war. Now, we were isolated again. There were no sources of help or information. On the other hand, the work conditions in Jędrzejów were very different from what I had experienced in my job at the smithy. We had to deal with new, different managers and guards. And the kind of labor that we did was definitely not skilled. Mostly, we unloaded gravel from freight cars. The gravel was for the railways' foundations. It was as if we were back in Konin or even worse.

Hans had told me that the treatment of the guards reflected what was happening on the war fronts. After every German defeat, the guards took revenge on us. There was a lot of truth in what he said.

We were watched very closely. We worked in a railway station and the guards were wary that we would try to escape. The food ration was the same as in Konin – the hot water called "soup" and a quarter of a loaf of bread. Fortunately for us and especially for me, we had recovered strength during the months we had been in Andrzejów. Thanks to that, we did not weaken immediately.

In the Jędrzejów camp I was involved in an interesting incident. One day a high rank SS officer and a company commander came to the camp in an armored open car. The guards had ordered us to work quicker without stopping in order to impress the visitors. At one point, the SS officer looked at us scornfully and asked if there was anyone among the dirty Jews who knew how to change a car wheel. There was silence. Our guard repeated the question and I whispered that I knew how to do it. The truth was that I had never actually done it. I had just seen how they did it in a Gombin garage. The guard took me to the SS officer and said that I could do it. He looked at me, asked how old I was and where I had learned to take care of cars. Then he warned me: "If you fail, you will be punished in front of everyone. I will consider it as an attempt on my life, so your life is in danger, is it clear?" I said: "Yes sir." Then I asked him to kindly show me where he kept the jack. Since he did not seem to understand, I explained that in order to change the wheel the car had to be lifted. It turned out that there was no jack.

I called other prisoners, we lifted the car and put it on wooden logs. I changed the wheel as fast as I could and we put the car down. As a token of gratitude, the officer slapped me twice and kicked me in the belly. Then he gave me another speech: "Your lives are spared. You are lucky that you managed to lift the car and did not fail in your task. Why should I carry a jack when we have dirty asses like you?"

He told our guard that I had done well and that he should give me some extra bread. The next day the guard brought me a whole loaf of bread with a herring. Our whole group celebrated my success eating those delicacies. The guard told me that I had been lucky because the officer really meant to carry out his threat. He thought that I did not understand to what extent the danger had been real. In his words: "the honor of an SS man binds him to keep his promises."

On that same day I was transferred to the workshops to do skilled labor, less stressing, no daily quotas and the most important benefit – the possibility of getting additional food from the Gentiles who worked there.

The incident showed how cheap our lives were. I was confident about my skills and I did not think that my life was at risk. But our guard quoted the SS officer: "the Jews always lie, there are no capable workers among them." That was the reason why he was surprised.

In the Jędrzejów camp we faced a torment that we had not experienced before: we were supposed to sleep on wooden planks with straw mattresses that were full of bugs, fleas and lice. The insects sucked our blood and we were covered with rashes and sores. Since we could not sleep, we were physically deteriorating. Many prisoners were completely exhausted.

One day, out of the blue, the Germans burned the mattresses and disinfected the shacks. We were sent to Łódź ghetto to be fumigated and take showers. Łódź was not far from the camp, just a few kilometers. We entered the ghetto under heavy guard. We were not allowed to speak with anyone. Since we saw women and children, we understood that not all the Jews had been deported from the Łódź ghetto. When we returned to the Jędrzejów camp we did not go to the shacks. Without any explanation, they loaded us on trucks and took us away.

# To an unknown destination

It was a short drive to the railway station where freight cars were waiting for us. They loaded us into the cars with shouts and beatings until there was no more standing room. After throwing inside half an empty barrel to serve as latrine, the guards locked the doors from outside. For long hours the cars stayed parked at the station. We did not receive food or drink. With dawn, the cars were moved to a different track and we started our journey, which took a day and a half.

Through the cracks in the walls of the car we could see open spaces and forests. It was hard to bear that we were locked in a cage like animals while outside there were green fields, grazing cows and farmers toiling their land. The longing for freedom was unbearable - we wanted to be like them.

The overcrowding inside the car was oppressive. The stench caused people to swoon and faint. The men were so tired that they fell asleep standing up, leaning on each other. Some of those who fainted did not wake up - they just died and we did not have room for laying them down. As time passed, the situation worsened.

At one of the stations we shouted loudly asking the guards to open the doors in order to remove the dead and empty the barrel. The guards fired in the air as a warning and, when the shouting did not stop, they began to shoot directly into the cars. Some of the men in our car were wounded. The floor was covered with blood.

We used the clothes of the dead to bandage the wounded. The SS seemed determined to exhaust us to death. They could have added cars to reduce the overcrowding and could have given us some minimal food and water, but they did not do that. They wanted us to arrive to our destination as weakened and exhausted as possible. We came to the conclusion that our end was near, despite the fact that we did not know yet for sure that there were mass-killing camps or, to be more precise, that the Germans were executing an extermination program for all the Jews.

After indescribable suffering we finally reached our destination. The train stopped and the doors opened. Trained dogs jumped on us and started tearing our clothes and flesh. We were told to jump out, line up on the side of the cars, and wait there. The noise and tumult were shocking. Lots of people were running around. Children crying for their parents, women looking for their children and husbands, everyone trying to find their relatives. There were SS officers organizing the crowd into three columns - one for men, one for women, and a third one for women with children. We did not understand their language but we knew that they were Jews because they wore patches with the yellow Star of David on their chests and their backs. We then found out that our arrival had coincided with the arrival of a transport of Jews from France and Belgium. We could see entire families. They had brought lots of luggage.

While standing there, we saw a cart loaded with weird-looking men. They were dressed with striped clothes, round flat hats, and wooden clogs. On the left side of their chest they had a triangle-shaped patch with a number. We soon realized that it was a work team that dealt with the luggage. They collected the suitcases and bags, loaded them on the carts, and took them away for sorting. The prisoners of that team were a sorry sight. We immediately knew that we had to expect very hard times. From what we heard them say, we learned that we had arrived at Auschwitz.

*Yitzhak Weizman*

# PART II

*Yitzhak Weizman*

# Auschwitz[3]

Auschwitz was the biggest and deadliest of the concentration camps established by the Germans to enact their "final solution" for the European Jews. The railway station was far from the camp and had been especially built for the reception of the human transports and the selection of those who would be slave workers for a while and those who would immediately die in the gas chambers.

We were still standing where we got off the train. From the distance we saw the long lines. Young men were sent to the right, older men to the left. On the line of women with children we saw heartbreaking scenes when the children were separated from their mothers. Most of the women went with their children despite the fact that they had another choice. They understood that the fate of the children would be different from that of the men and women who were able to work.

The SS officers lied brazenly at the railway station. They still claimed that the children would take showers and go to sanatoriums and schools until the end of the war. They would come back safe and healthy.

I will never forget the viciousness, cruelty, and inhumanity of those scenes. In my mind, I visualized the agonizing moment when I was torn from the arms of my mother and my sister a year before.

After some time the turmoil subsided. The Germans completed the process of sorting out the transport from France, aligned the columns of people, and took them away to their different destinations. Our

---

[3] Editor's note] The precise date of Yitzhak Weizman's arrival in Auschwitz-Birkenau can be established on the basis of the number that was assigned to him and tattooed on his arm. His number, 145227, corresponds to a train transport that arrived on September 2, 1943. Polish Holocaust historian Danuta Czech, who combed the camp's archives and wrote a daily chronicle of events in Auschwitz-Birkenau, summarized the fate of the passengers as follows: "After selection, 788 men, who receive numbers from 144491 to 145278, and 42 women, who are registered with numbers from 57855 to 57896, are interned in the camp. The other people, about 2170, are killed in the gas chambers." Source: Danuta Czech, *Kalendarium der Ereignisse im Konzentrationslager Auschwitz-Birkenau, 1939-1945 [Calendar of Events in the Concentration Camp Auschwitz-Birkenau, 1939-1945]*, Rowohlt Verlag, Hamburg, 2008, p. 593.

34

Men, women and children step out of an overcrowded train at the Birkenau ramp. The chimneys of two crematorium buildings are visible on the horizon. Image source: Yad Vashem.

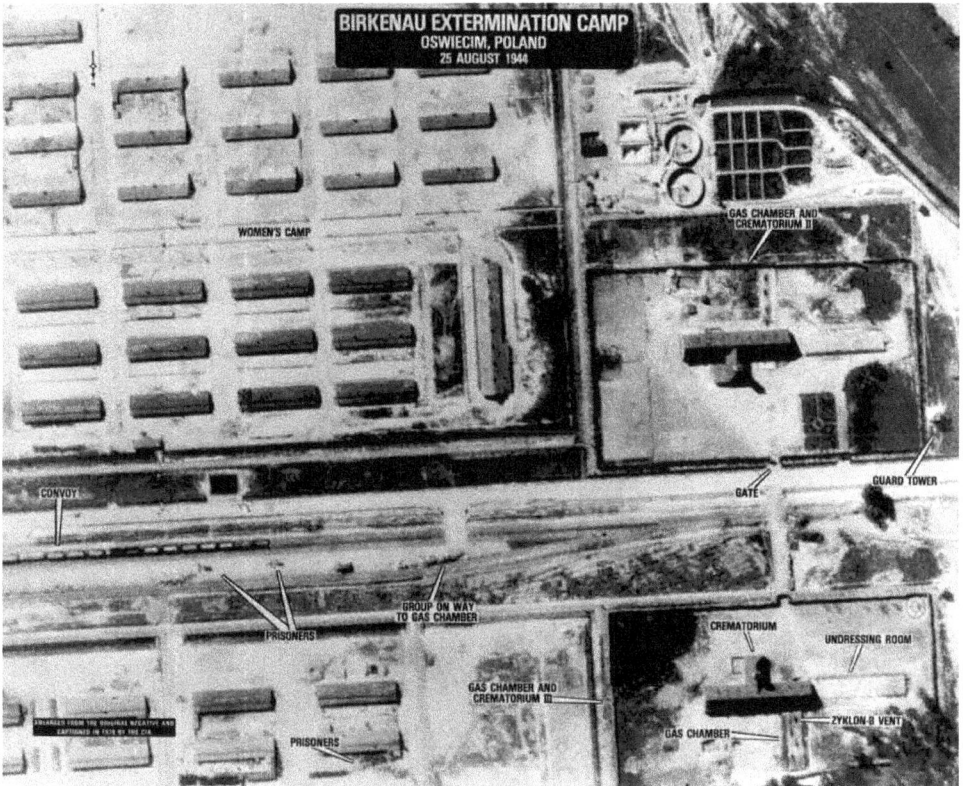

BIRKENAU EXTERMINATION CAMP
OSWIECIM, POLAND
25 AUGUST 1944

WOMEN'S CAMP

GAS CHAMBER AND CREMATORIUM II

CONVOY

GATE

GUARD TOWER

GROUP ON WAY TO GAS CHAMBER

PRISONERS

CREMATORIUM

UNDRESSING ROOM

GAS CHAMBER AND CREMATORIUM III

PRISONERS

GAS CHAMBER

ZYKLON-B VENT

Enlarged section of an aerial photograph taken by a Mosquito plane of the South African Air Force. It grimly illustrates the author's description of the "processing" of incoming human transports, showing the gas chambers and crematoriums, a train by the platform, a large group of people on their way to the gas chambers, and the prisoners left behind after their selection for work. Image source: Yad Vashem (closer visualization in Yad Vashem's webpage "Aerial Photographs of Auschwitz": https://www.yadvashem.org/yv/en/exhibitions/through-the-lens/auschwitz-aerial-photos.asp).

turn came. After receiving the information about our transport, the head of the SS came to us. He said that we were going to work hard and that we had to be fit for it. Did anyone need rest or medical attention? Nobody said a word. Even the wounded kept quiet. After a short wait, the officer conducted his own selection. They loaded the sick and weak on a truck and ordered the rest of us to start walking.

We marched for about an hour until we reached the camp's gate. From a distance we saw the sign ARBEIT MACHT FREI (work makes you free). We knew that we were approaching a huge camp because we walked for a long time along an electrified fence with concrete posts and watchtowers equipped with machine guns and powerful searchlights. Inside the camp there were huge wooden barracks arranged in endless rows. We noticed that the camp had separate zones for men and women. We reached the gate exhausted and hungry. They gave us the food ration of "soup" and a quarter of a loaf of bread.

# Birkenau

We had arrived at twilight. It was before roll call, after which nobody was allowed out of the barracks. Anyone caught outside risked being flogged or deprived of his food ration.

The hubbub in the camp was grotesque. The prisoners were dressed in striped clothing, frightfully thin, hardly dragging their legs. It was hard to distinguish one from the other – they all looked like skeletons. We were scared stiff by the thought that our fate would be the same. But I did not allow myself to get depressed. I was prepared for the worst. Despite my fatigue, feebleness and hunger I made an effort to avoid falling into apathy. My power of resistance was weakening, but I did not want to give up.

I asked around about conditions in the camp, but I got no answers. I was only told that I was lucky to be in the work zone - the other areas of the camp were just for selection and transport.

They took us to one of the barracks, so high and long that one could not see where it ended. In the middle of the barrack there was a rectangular structure that was supposed to be a heating oven, but it was never operated. Lengthwise, the barrack was a series of sections that had a couple of three-level wooden bunks on each side. The space between the planks was very narrow – one had to crawl to get in. There was no bedding, no mattresses, not even straw. Lying down was uncomfortable because of the wide gaps between the plank boards. We were told that we would receive a blanket, but we never did.

Suddenly a deafening siren was heard signaling that we had to report for roll call. We stood by the bunks until the guards finished counting and recording attendance. The guards were SS men from an especially cruel "elite" unit. They bolted the doors from outside. We were locked in until the next morning.

Before entering the barrack some prisoners had managed to get bits of information about our new place. We were in a camp called Birkenau, adjacent to the main Auschwitz camp. They also received this important advice: "you should never eat your whole bread ration when you receive it in the evening." The ration was for a day. If we gulped it down we would have to work for the entire next day without food, enduring hunger until the evening. One of the men lying on the plank beneath me heard that before the war the whole area had been a big camp of the Polish army. The buildings of Auschwitz had been used as officers' quarters and the Birkenau barracks as the horse stables of the cavalry force. The barrack looked indeed like a place for horses. The Polish army had built the heating ovens to warm the horses in winter. The Germans never operated them.

In the Birkenau camp, there were three sub-camps for the people who had been selected as able-bodied and capable of work. In one of them were the men - mostly Jews, some German political prisoners, and Russian prisoners of war (wounded Russians were sent straight to the gas chambers like the Jews who were not selected for work). The second sub-camp was for women – mostly Jewish and a few female political prisoners. The third sub-camp was for Gypsies, who were treated worse than the Jews. The three sub-camps were separated by double electric fences with watchtowers and searchlights.

I fell asleep on the plank while still listening to the information, without any covering and without taking off my clogs. But I frequently had to change my lying position because the gaps between the boards hurt dreadfully. That was how I passed my first day in the "paradise" called Birkenau.

The next morning at dawn they opened the doors and gave us fifteen minutes to wash and go to the latrines. Hundreds of men competed for access to the latrines and faucets. There was a nasty tumult. Not everyone was able to finish in that short time. Some of the men gave up because they had to run back to roll call.

The roll call was not only for counting but also for selection. We had to take off our clothes and stand naked in front of the SS. They split us into two groups – one group, including me, was sent back to the barrack, the other group was loaded on a truck. Among them were some people from Gombin. By then we already knew where they were going. The prisoners we met at Birkenau had confirmed what we had suspected all along - that the sick and weak were being exterminated by the Germans.

Once again I had faced death and had been spared. I tried to figure out why I was sent to the right while some of the people I knew were sent to the left. I could not find an answer. Even today I have no explanation. In some cases the differences in in physical condition were not pronounced. They were young like me, but they were sent to extermination.

The circle of my friends and acquaintances was narrowing. I will never forget the parting. I can still see their waving hands as they stood on the truck naked, frozen and shivering. The look on their faces said it all. Some of them raised their hands and cried Shma Israel (Hear, O Israel). As I said, we knew already what would happen to them. In they would be dead in less than fifteen minutes. Not far from the camp there were gas chambers disguised as showers. They were taken there. I could not absorb it. It was unbelievable.

That same day they took us to the "clinic" where numbers were tattooed on our left arms, numbers that would remain engraved forever. My number was 145227. The tattooing hurt terribly. Mixed with the ink, my blood flowed from the pricks of the needle. It felt like a very painful burn. They told us to let it dry and refrain from touching or wiping it.

After registration, we received striped clothes, including a striped hat. On the chest of the garment was the letter P (for our country of origin) and the number that had been tattooed on our arm. We spent the entire day without food. Only when all the arrangements were finished they gave us our first ration of hot water and a quarter of a loaf of bread. On that first day we did not work. After that, we spent a year and a half working continuously, seven days a week from dawn to sunset.

I was assigned to a workshop where crashed airplanes brought from the front were dismantled. It was not far from the camp and we went there on foot. In that same area there were several other workshops in which prisoners worked.

I started on a routine of suffering, hunger and continuous torment by fleas and lice. They sucked our blood day and night. My body shrank as it tried to adapt to the meager ration of food. In Auschwitz it was impossible to obtain additional food, even if you had money. Like some of the others, I still had the valuables that I had kept hidden in the sewed pockets of my old clothes (when we changed clothes upon arrival, I had managed to slip the valuables into the pockets of my striped garments). But when I tried to buy rations of bread I could not find sellers. My treasure was simply worthless.

It was very dangerous to keep valuables. I witnessed the hanging of a prisoner because he was caught with stuff when he was going out to work. He had collected jewelry and diamonds while sorting the clothes of new arrivals. Later on, he was assigned to work in painting. He dropped the treasure in a pail full of paint and tried his luck at the gate. He planned to bury the valuables in the working area outside the camp, hoping to be a rich man if he survived. It was not clear how the ruse had been discovered. He may have looked suspicious or perhaps someone reported him. In any case, when he reached the gate he was removed from the line, while the others kept marching in tune with the music that was played every morning by the orchestra. They hung him in front of all of us when we returned from work.

I remember the trains that came in mid-1943 from Warsaw Ghetto. By then, there were incoming transports from all over Poland and the other occupied countries. We knew about every train that arrived in Birkenau – number of wagons, number of people, and countries of origin. We got the details from the prisoners who collected the suitcases and bags at the railway station. Time and again, they saw the procedure from the moment the trains arrived. Most of the people went straight to the gas chambers - only a small proportion was selected for work in the camp.

The prisoners that worked at the train station brought lots of goods into the camp, including the valuables and food that they found in the luggage. They smuggled the stuff into the camp using risky methods. One day, we heard that it was possible to buy food from them in a particular barrack. We confirmed that it was true when we saw some men furtively sharing a loaf of moldy black bread in our barrack. They told us whom to approach to buy food. I talked with a couple of trusted friends and we decided to pool our valuables and try our luck. We agreed that I would be in charge of the purchase - being the youngest, I was less likely to be suspected of carrying valuables. We sealed our pact with a handshake and I went out. However, just when I was about to reach the other barrack, I suddenly heard the siren for roll call. I had to stop in my tracks and return to our barrack.

On my way back a young SS stopped me. He yelled: "What are you doing outside?" Without waiting for an answer he dragged me to the nearest barrack, ordered me to kneel down, and gave me fifteen lashes with a thick stick. The pain was wrenching but I had to endure it. I was scared to death that the valuables would spill out of my pocket during the flogging. With my outmost will power I took the punishment in silence. When he was done, the SS astonished me saying that he would escort me to my barrack. He added: "Otherwise you may be caught and punished again by the guards." I raised my face and we exchanged looks. He understood that I thanked him.

That was how I returned, frightened and humiliated but alive and breathing. My friends could not believe their eyes. They hugged me, glad that I was still alive. They told me: "We thought that we would not see you again. It was a miracle from heaven that he did not notice the valuables. Some power is protecting you."

A prisoner whom I did not know very well approached me and said: "If you add the digits of the number on your arm you will find that the sum is twenty-one. You have a lucky number - you were chosen to stay alive." In our conditions, we longed for some hope. I started to believe that there might be something in what he said.

My friends told me: "We were right in choosing you for the task. It did not occur to the SS man that a small lad was carrying anything." They were older and taller than me, and it was probably true that they would have been suspected of something more serious than just being late for roll call. After calming down, I thought about it and understood how much I had endangered myself. I had once again received my life back.

As time went on, we continued to lose strength. I was in better physical shape than most of my mates, but I cannot offer an explanation for that. Some prisoners committed suicide. They could not take any more suffering. They walked to the electric fence, grabbed the wires and died. They preferred death to the fear of waiting for the next selection and being sent to the gas chambers. As I said, the fate of the children, their mothers, the sick and the weak was no longer a secret. We could see the flames that came out of the crematorium chimneys at night. A permanent smell of burned bodies floated in the air.

There was a group of prisoners, the Sonderkommando (special squad), that slept in a separate barrack and received better food. They worked in the crematoriums. They had to open the gas chambers, take out the bodies and load them on carts that went straight to the ovens. Later they loaded the ashes on trucks and dumped them into the Vistula river, always escorted by armed guards.

I remember the deed of two Greek Jews who were in the Sonderkommando. Taking advantage of a distraction of their German guard at the dumping site, they hit him with their shovels, grabbed his gun and killed him. Then they jumped into the river and swam to the other side in an attempt to escape. When they realized what was going on, the Germans returned the other prisoners to the camp and launched a search. The fugitives were found and executed. Their bodies were put on display to teach us the lesson. For us, however, they were heroes.

As further punishment, the Germans conducted a particularly strict selection on that same day. Hundreds were sent to the gas chambers. For the Germans it was very important to catch runaway prisoners. It was not just a matter of inflicting exemplary punishments to prevent escape attempts. They also wanted to maintain secrecy. Anyone who escaped was an eyewitness who could tell the world about the industry of death in Auschwitz.

Only someone from the Sonderkommando could think about escaping. Compared to the rest of us, they were in better physical shape. Since they were not totally wasted by hunger, they could entertain the idea. The other reason, as mentioned above, had to do with their work. The dumping of ashes was organized in such a way that there was only one truck at a time by the river. Each truck had a driver and a guard, so the prisoners had a chance to overcome the guard and escape swimming. In any case, what they did proves that not everyone went like "cattle to the slaughter."

There was another heroic deed. A young woman from France was walking with the others towards the gas chambers. There were SS men escorting the crowd. The young woman snatched the pistol from the holster of one of them and shot him to death. Another SS shot her but, before dying, she managed to return the fire and hit him. The Sonderkommando prisoners who saw the incident told us about it.

The fact that some people fought back encouraged us. We felt the desire for revenge in our guts. Every act of resistance was punished on the spot and many paid with their lives. They hanged ten women in the camp's square as a reprisal for the young woman's action.

During the first months of 1944, we began to notice that most of the new arrivals were Jews from Hungary. The number of transports increased and there was a rapid population turnover in the camp. The selections went on and on, one barrack after another. More prisoners were assigned to work in the train station and we heard that they had finished building a fourth crematorium. Every morning on our way to work we passed near the gigantic crematoriums. We saw the fire and smoke that came out of the chimneys and smelled the burned flesh. The German guards said that they were soap factories for the army, but we knew the truth.

With the increased frequency of transports, the Germans added a third shift and the crematoriums operated through the entire night. The wind brought the full strength of the stench to our barracks and the fire from the chimneys rose several meters high, like a cry to heaven. Week after week we saw the extermination with our own eyes. We were sure that we were doomed. It was unthinkable that the Germans would allow any eyewitnesses to leave that place alive.

By the end of that year, the SS who took us to work were replaced by older guards. We began to sense that something was happening. There was less pressure at work. We got some rest and received a bigger food ration. The vigilance was less tight. One day, two men from our group vanished. They had prepared a place to hide and, from there, they managed to escape. It was a daring, unprecedented feat.

The area where we worked was huge. It had lots of warehouses and workshops. Thousands of crashed airplanes and piles of junk were scattered all over the place. It was easy to find a hiding place. The real problem was how to hold on until the Germans stopped the search. It required having enough food and water and counting on external help to be able to run away and find shelter.

It was obvious that the prisoners' escape had been very well-planned. It must have involved a large sum of money, considering that they were helped by people who were inside and outside the camp. The Germans mobilized a large force, put up roadblocks and ran searches around the camp and its surroundings. But we never heard that the prisoners had been caught. To this day I do not know what became of them.

Like the others in the group that dismantled airplanes, I was very worried. We knew what the Germans did when someone tried to escape. We expected a cruel retaliation.

On that same day all of us were individually interrogated. The methods they used included beatings, bayonet stabbings, flogging, and kicks in the groin. They were especially interested in the guards and in the German political prisoners who worked with us. Names were read to us, asking if we had any contacts with them. There was an element of random luck in those interrogations. Some were more heavily tortured than others. I got lashes and kicks, but did not suffer as much as some of my mates. The interrogations went on until nightfall, when they brought us back to the camp. We went to sleep without receiving our food rations – the punishment that was probably most effective to break our morale.

Our feelings about the escape were ambivalent. We wished the fugitives success and hoped that they would be able to spread the word about the mass murders in Auschwitz. At the same time, we resented the fact that they knew that the other prisoners would have to pay for their escape.

That night, all those who had valuables hid them in the unused oven that stood in the middle of our barrack. We expected that the Germans would conduct a thorough search on the following day, but we were in for a surprise. They did not show up to take us to work in the morning.

By noon, we heard the siren and entered the barrack for roll call. Frightened and tensed, we stood waiting for what was coming. After a while, a group of SS arrived with a distinguished looking high-rank officer. They ordered us to take off our clothes and stand naked in single line. We immediately knew that it was going to be an unforgiving selection because, after our first selection on arrival, they had never told us again to stand naked – they just did it by our general looks.

Some of the prisoners tried to hide under the bunks. The SS men shot them on the spot. They were taken out and loaded on the truck that was waiting outside. It was snowing and the temperature was below zero. Dead and wounded were thrown on top of each other and the blood flowing from the truck reddened the snow. The wounded were finished off with a bullet to the head.

That dreadful scene is deeply engraved in my memory.

We stood naked awaiting our destiny. A group of SS were standing by near the door of the barrack. The selection started. We were called one by one and inspected by the SS high-rank officer. Later we learned that he was the notorious Josef Mengele, who conducted horrible medical experiments in the camp.

The selection was implacable. It was enough to have the smallest scratch to be sent to the left, which meant outside to the truck and the gas chamber. It was obvious that prisoners in miserable hygienic conditions would have wounds, boils and scratches. That was how a lot of people were sent to extermination that day.

The selection went on and soon it would be my turn. There was only one prisoner before me in the line. When he was called, he hesitated. Another yell and he still stood frozen. I bypassed him and advanced towards the SS high-rank officer. He gave me a quick look and sent me to the right.

I was spared again. The hesitator was sent to the gas chambers. None of that was premeditated. I acted instinctively, like an animal in fear of death.

Mengele was supposed to "scientifically" diagnose who was weak and exhausted. The truth was that there was almost no difference in the state of the prisoners. All of us were just a twisted bag of skin and bones. The main differences were in the condition of our skins. It was on that basis that he decided who would die and who would be allowed to go on living.

Following the selection, we stayed in the camp cleaning the latrines and collecting the garbage. The fact that they did not send us back to dismantle airplanes worried us – it meant that we were less useful for them.

The collection of garbage took us close to the women's camp. Their looks shocked us. Their heads were shaven and we noticed by their behavior that some of them were demented. Like many of the men, they had been driven insane by starvation, disease, and ruthless labor.

We were approaching the end of 1944 and we did not know what was happening on the front. We could only guess by what was going on in the camp. The men who worked in projects that were vital for the war effort told us that there was less production and even partial idleness. On the other hand, the transports kept coming and the crematoriums were active around the clock. The fog and the stench fanned out through the camp and chocked us to breathlessness.

We wondered about the Poles who lived in the area. They saw things and smelled the stench. They surely knew what was happening, but they kept silent. Later we learned that, in addition to Auschwitz-Birkenau, there were dozens of extermination sites throughout Poland. Nobody protested or reported it. The fact that anti-Semitism was so deeply rooted among the Poles must have played a role in the Germans' decision to carry out the "final solution" in their country. The silence of the Poles proved their indifference to the extermination of the Jews.

By then, the bulk of the new workers were young men from Hungary. Most of them could only speak Hungarian, a language that sounded very alien to us. Only a few knew Yiddish or German – those who came from Mukaczewo (or Munkacs in Hungarian). It was difficult to communicate with them, but they managed to tell us that the Germans were retreating in Russia and that the American and English armies were approaching Germany from France. Knowing that Germany was losing the war gave us some hope, but we were still convinced that they would not leave eyewitnesses alive. They were going to finish us off at the last moment.

Most of the people arriving from Hungary were sent to the gas chambers. When those transports stopped coming, there was a drastic change. Many of us were no longer working. We walked aimlessly around the camp without roll calls or any kind of schedule. It was disturbing because it was unconceivable that the Germans would keep feeding the Jews for nothing in return. The rumors were rampant, mostly predicting our doom.

As the Russian front got closer, the Germans began to empty the camp. The selections started again. The same notorious doctor came to our barrack. I felt numb. This time we were not told to take off our clothes. We simply faced the examiners near the main door. Some prisoners were ordered to stand and wait outside, while the others had to climb into trucks. When my turn came, Mengele looked at me and asked my age. "Sixteen," I responded. "He looks well but he is small," he said to his helper. "Check his height." The helper took my measure and I was below the threshold. They sent me to the trucks outside and that was it. I cannot remember what I though or felt.

When the selection was over the trucks drove away. Since there had not been enough room for everybody, some of us had to wait for another truck. After a while, they told us to start walking towards the main gate. Knowing that we were going to the gas chambers, we walked slowly, stopping from time to time. Some in our group begged to be killed. Others lifted their hands and shouted: "Our God in heaven, where are you? Help us, do not abandon us." The SS guards beat us murderously and shot in the air. After a half-hour walk we reached the gate, but we were stalled by what seemed to be a dispute about the exit permit. Within minutes, two officers showed up in an open command car. They wore elegant uniforms with shining boots. The guards saluted them and there was a brief exchange. Then, our guards returned with an order to take us back to the barracks. We did not know who the officers were or why the order was given.

Since we had been already sorted and marked, we were at a loss to understand whether or not we had been saved from death. We later learned that, probably obeying orders from a higher authority, the camp commander had told the gate guards that the groups of people going to the gas chambers should be stopped and sent back.

We spent the next few days in a state of doubt and anxiety. Being idle, we had plenty of time for the most pessimistic speculations. We knew that the selections had ceased and that the groups remaining in the camp were not working. We felt that the end was near. No other possibility occurred to us.

Eventually, they began to load us on trucks without any selection - all of us with no exception. When we started moving, someone said: "In a few minutes we will know... If we turn left when we pass the gate, it is the gas chambers. If we turn to the right, only God knows where we are going."

The truck passed the gate and turned to the right. A glimmer of hope. Perhaps we were not going to die. The feeling was reinforced by the fact that it was a long drive. We finally arrived to a small railway station where they transferred us to freight cars. Since it was not too crowded we lied down on the floor.

We stayed at the station for long hours, unnerved by the smoking chimney that we had seen on the roof of the rear car. Were the

Germans planning some devious trick?  They had given us a ration of bread, but they had not provided a bucket to relieve ourselves, so we assumed that the journey would be short.

## **Stutthof**[4]

At nightfall, we started moving. The train raced fast all through the night. Next morning we were hundreds of kilometers away from Auschwitz, but we did not know our destination. Then the train stopped in an isolated spot. We saw expanses of green fields with high wheat and other crops but not buildings. They opened the doors and told us to step down in groups of ten. We were surprised when they distributed plates and cups and took us to the rear car, where we received a hot drink that tasted somewhat like coffee. Only then the mystery of the chimney was solved – the rear car was a field kitchen on wheels.

We were startled by their treatment. They allowed us to relieve ourselves in the field, of course under strict guarding. We still worried about our destination, but some of us thought that our treatment signaled a basic policy change. Had they wanted to kill us, they would not have sent us on such a long trip with a field kitchen attached to the train.

We reckoned that we had crossed the entire length of Poland from south to north. At dawn the train began to slow down. Through the cracks in the walls of the car we intermittently saw built areas and open spaces.

The train stopped near a big forest. We smelled the pines and breathed a lungful of good air. To the right of the forest there was a small camp, about ten wooden structures surrounded by fences and watchtowers. We noticed that there were no chimneys. It was a tough walk to the camp. It was raining, the soil was muddy, and our clogs stuck in the mud.

We reached the gate completely exhausted. It was early morning. We saw prisoners holding food utensils, some in civilian clothes and others with striped garments. The guards at the gate told us that we were in Stutthof. The camp was located near Danzig, the port city on

---

[4] [Editor's note] Yitzhak Weizman's prisoner card indicates that he arrived in Stutthof concentration camp on October 28, 1944. He was registered as prisoner number 100250. Source: Arolsen Archives, Incarceration Documents, Stutthof Concentration Camp, Personal Files, Icek Wajcman's prisoner card, T/D Nr. 392471, Umschlog-Nr. 43952.

the Baltic Sea that had been in dispute between Poland and Germany before the war. The Polish name of the city was Gdansk.

We had been right in our guess about the northern direction of our journey. Now we could evaluate our situation. First, we were hundreds of kilometers away from Auschwitz, the most horrifying hell on earth. Second, we were no longer in Poland. Danzig had been annexed to the Reich, not as occupied territory but as a German city.

The fact that we were on German soil gave us hope, but our condition had not changed - we were still prisoners. We were still in the universe of those weird-looking men whose first sight had astounded me. People who looked like ghosts, heads sunk in their necks, and noses that seemed grotesquely long because of their extreme emaciation. Stooped old men who shivered from the cold and walked slowly, shuffling their legs in a deep state of apathy. The camp prisoners called them "Muselmann" because they wandered around with hunched backs and covered with blankets (evoking the image of the Muslims' robes and their prostrated posture during prayers). Being a "Muselmann" implied that you had reached the lowest stage of human degradation in the camps. Looking at each other, we almost lost the will to go on living. We ourselves looked like walking skeletons.

Immediately upon arrival in Stutthof there was a roll call. Some people had died on the train and others on the day we arrived. After checking and counting we were taken to wash by troughs that were arranged in parallel rows in the open air. There were no faucets – just holes in the pipes that trickled droplets of water. All of us tried to reach the troughs. The strongest were able to wet their faces. The weaker stayed behind.

After the "wash" we lined up and received half a loaf of bread. We were ecstatic. It was the largest ration we had received in two years. Was it a one-time giveaway? Just in case, we abstained from eating it all on the spot. As we had learned to do, we saved something for the next day. We had become "experts" in apportioning our food rations. We kept the bread pieces safeguarded in our pockets and struggled to overcome temptation. Despite the agonizing hunger, we did not touch those precious crumbs of bread until we were about to receive the next ration.

We talked with prisoners who had arrived in the previous days. They were Jews from Lithuania and Latvia who had been in other camps. They confirmed that the Russians were advancing toward Poland. They also told us that, from Stutthof, people were sent to work camps in Germany. We were doubtful about that information. It was unlikely that we, Auschwitz-Birkenau "graduates," would be transferred to Germany. It was hard for us to be optimistic. Still, I began to think that maybe the worst part of the war was behind us. If the information turned out to be true, it would give new meaning to our struggle for survival.

The Lithuanian and Latvian prisoners knew nothing about the extermination in Auschwitz. Did they believe the stories we told them? I was not sure. Perhaps they did not have the mental disposition to show any feeling about our stories. Like us, they could not understand how the Germans allowed us to leave that cursed hell.

It was the first time that I met people whose Yiddish was different from ours. I felt attuned to it. The Lithuanian Yiddish has pleasant inflections and includes many Hebrew words. I liked the language and tried to imitate it. It sounded more authentic than our Yiddish, which was mixed with many Polish words.

During the two years that I had been away from home I had never been sick. In Stutthof, however, I inadvertently scratched my hand. The next morning, I woke up with high fever. I felt weak and saw a red streak that stretched up from the wound through the whole length of my arm. The older prisoners said that it was an infection. If it reached my heart I would be in great danger because I was too undernourished and weak to fight the infection. My mates discussed the situation. Should the guard in charge be informed or should we try to find a different solution? We knew what the Germans did with the sick in the camps.

I was frightened and depressed. My optimism was gone. Just when there was a spark of hope I was sick. I did not feel much physical pain, but I could hardly stand on my feet and the anxiety was wearing me down. Luckily, my childhood friend from Gombin, Lajzer Bocian, found a Lithuanian Jew who could help. In exchange for a whole loaf of bread, he would take me to a friend of his who worked in the infirmary as an assistant. I agreed and we went to look for his friend. He checked my hand and, without saying a word, took a needle from his coat collar and made an incision in the wound. After the pus drained out, he applied a black lotion, bandaged my hand and arm, and took off before I had time to thank him. On the way out he said: "This is the most I can do for you, I have no other means, and neither does the doctor."

The lotion worked like magic. The red streak began to vanish and by the next day it was gone. The fever went down and I felt much better. I was still weak but immensely relieved. My friends said: "Now we really believe in your lucky number."

Later we learned that also in Stutthof there was a small crematorium to dispose of the dead. Fortunately, they did not put us to work. That helped my recovery. Otherwise, I would not have survived. For us, Stutthof was a transit camp. After two weeks they took us away without any selections.

# In transit

The winter of 1944-1945 brought lots of snow and mud. We knew that the Germans were withdrawing on all fronts. Their defeat was certain, but they still treated us as sub-humans. We were again crowded like cattle in the cars of a train. The small windows were sealed with wood boards. It was dark, stifling and stinking. We could not peep out and it was difficult to breathe. The conditions were so bad that it was difficult to believe that they were taking us to work. But as the train gained speed, the ventilation improved and those who had fainted were able to recover.

As we got deeper into Germany the train slowed down and stopped often. There were obstacles on the way. We frequently heard airplanes and the fire of anti-aircraft guns. The prisoners that stood by the window had managed to partially release one of the boards. They moved it up to allow air to came in and to look outside. During one of the stops we saw anti-aircraft posts manned by boys of the Hitler Jugend (the Nazi youth movement). For us, it was proof that the Germans were in really bad shape.

Our train was targeted several times by bombers and fighter planes. Some bombs fell quite close and the cars were hit by machine-gun fire. One prisoner was wounded in the palm of his hand by a splinter that penetrated the car. He was about my age and one of his fingers was paralyzed. It was sad because he played the piano before the war and had dreamed about a musical career.

It took two days to reach our destination. The car doors opened to the usual "welcoming" reception: yelling, swearing and blows. We went straight to roll call.

# Fuel manufacturing [Dautmergen][5]

A strong smell penetrated our noses, but it was different from the stench in Birkenau. It was oil or some other kind of fuel. A cloud of fire raised to the sky. Our eyes burned. None of this was good news. The cars had stopped near the camp, which was a hangar surrounded by a double barbed-wire fence with watchtowers in the four corners. The hangar was packed with prisoner "beds" – the familiar planks arranged on top of each other, with ladders for reaching the higher levels.

When we arrived we met some sick prisoners who had not gone to work that day. They looked the same as us. We were all extremely thin and worn out. They gave us details about our new camp. It was a factory that used some new invention to produce synthetic fuel out of shale oil or brown coal. During the war, the shortages of fuel were huge. Most of the German trucks operated on gas that was produced by burning wood. The trucks were started with regular fuel and shifted to gas when the engine warmed up. They were fitted with a big wood boiler and the gas was injected into the engine.

The factory was a priority target. There were constant air raids. The Allies made every effort to destroy it. We had hardly managed to get organized when we witnessed one of the routine attacks of the

---

[5] [Editor's note] Yitzhak Weizman could not recall the names of the last two camps where he worked in Germany. The information contained in his prisoner cards identify them as Dautmergen (work in a fuel manufacturing plant) and Hailfingen (work in a quarry). Both camps were part of the huge Natzweiler concentration complex, which included dozens of satellite camps on both sides of the Rhine in France and Germany. The Dautmergen camp prisoners worked in a project to extract synthetic fuel from oil shale deposits in Württemberg. The dates in Yitzhak Weizman's prisoner cards indicate that he was in Dautmergen between February 14, 1945 and April 12, 1945. Sources: *The KZ-Außenlager (subcamp) at the Night-Fighter Airbase Hailfingen/Tailfingen*, p. 41; Volker Mall et al, *Die Häftlinge des KZ-Außenlagers Hailfingen/Tailfingen [The prisoners of the concentration camp Hailfingen/Tailfingen]*, Herrenberg, 2020, Volume 2, p. 112; Arolsen Archives, Incarceration Documents, Dachau Concentration Camp, Office Cards, Itzek Wajcman's prisoner card, Nr. 156199.

plant. Our hangar, which was distant from the plant itself, was not bombed.

The discipline was severe because of the strategic importance and secrecy of the plant. Rather than SS men, our guards were veterans from a special Wehrmacht unit. They demanded full performance in the fulfillment of the daily outputs. It was a nearly impossible demand, but they had an efficient method to make us exert ourselves to the limit. Instead of beatings and torture, they gave us food rations that varied according to the daily output. That way, we had no choice but to do our outmost to meet the targets and get our full rations of food.

The Germans did not spare us the time that was lost to the air raids. We had to take cover, but immediately after the attacks they sent us back to work and kept us going until we finished the quota for the day. In any case, it was a satisfaction to see panic in the faces of the "superior race" when they ran with us to take shelter in the ditches. They showed more fear than we did. In those situations their stupidity and ugliness were revealed and they would not stare straight into our eyes. Their vulnerability encouraged us, despite the fact that they took us as scapegoats to vent their anxiety and anger. There were cases in which they got first to the ditches and drew their guns to keep us out. Some of them cursed the Allies, but others blamed Hitler and the Wehrmacht. We were scared of the raids, but we also saw them as a welcome sign that the Allies were close. The planes flew so low that we could see the pilots and the British markings on the wings.

In addition to Jews, there were many Russian prisoners working in the plant. All through our stay, the hangar where we lived was not bombed. The pilots knew that the slave workers were there and did not target it. We were aware of that, so much so that on some occasions the prisoners preferred to stay in the hangar rather than going out to receive the daily food ration.

There was not a day in which we did not face danger of death in the fuel plant. We finally understood why they had brought us from Auschwitz. For the Germans it was essential to produce fuel at any price, and our lives were certainly cheap.

The intensification of the raids had a softening effect on some guards. I heard one of them saying this to a prisoner: "You will soon be free. There are signs, but I am not allowed to tell you. I hope that you have a good opinion of me. I was a decent guard. All of us have the same wish – we want the war to end so that everybody can return to their families." On the whole, however, our treatment did not change. Not that it mattered – at that point, we did not have mental strength to think about settling accounts with the Germans.

In the end, the air raids were so effective that the plant could not continue to operate. Many prisoners had been killed or wounded. The installations were utterly smashed, to the point that reconstruction was impossible. We stopped going to work and spent several days in the hangar. The planes kept coming, flying in circles over the plant, probably taking photographs. Finally, everything was quiet. They took us in open trucks to yet another forced labor camp.

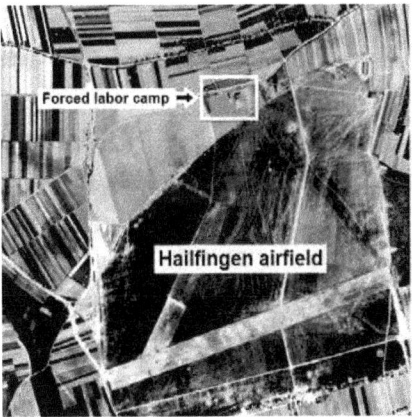

Aerial photograph of the Hailfingen military airfield taken by a reconnaissance plane of the US Air Force. The enlarged section on the right shows the installations of the forced labor camp. Image source: Gedenkstätte Hailfingen.

Number book of Natzweiler concentration camp complex showing Yitzhak Waizman (40990) among the men sent to Hailfingen subcamp. Image source: Arolsen Archives.

At the western end of the former airfield, the community of Hailfingen dedicated a memorial to the Jewish victims in 2010. The names of the 601 Jewish prisoners at the Hailfingen camp, including those who perished and the survivors, are engraved on the triangular monument. Image source: Gedenkstätte Hailfingen.

Entrance to the Dautmergen camp after the end of the war. Image source: Privatarchiv Immo Opfermann, *Gedenkstätten Rundschau*, Nr. 24, April 2020, p. 1.

Dautmergen camp aerial photograph, US Air Force, 15 Feb 1945. Image source: *Gedenkstätten Rundschau*, Nr. 24, April 2020, p. 7.

Monument to the victims of "Operation Wüste" in Schömberg's cemetery. Image source: Gedenkstätte Dautmergen-Schömberg.

Yitzhak Weizman's name in the list of prisoners from Dautmergen who arrived in Dachau-Allach on April 12, 1945). Image source: Arolsen Archives.

## Entrance test [Hailfingen]⁶

The drive was not long. We arrived to a forsaken village whose name I cannot remember. We got off the trucks near a forest covered with snow. The road was muddy. There were several shacks hidden in the forest, with the same fences and watchtowers that we had seen in the other camps. We did not expect better conditions. We were simply relieved that it was a work camp and not, heaven forbid, one of the Jews' final destinations.

We went through roll call, counting, registration, and assignment to one of the shacks. Near the entrance door we received the soup-like hot water before they locked us up. We waited for the next day. What would it bring?

With the first light they took us out of the shacks for roll call. Then they took us to work without wash, drink or food. The guards were brutal, yelling and kicking those could not keep up with the pace. Those who collapsed were just left behind lying in the mud and snow. After an exhausting march we reached our new place of work.

---

⁶ The name of this camp, which also eluded Yitzhak Weizman's memory, was Hailfingen. It was located in a Luftwaffe airfield that the Germans were reconditioning for use by night-fighter airplanes. The Jewish prisoners worked in two nearby stone quarries that supplied materials for the airfield's construction works. The dates in Yitzhak Weizman's prisoner cards specify that he was in Hailfingen between November 19, 1944 and February 14, 1945. Sources: Arolsen Archives, Registration of Foreigners and German Persecutees, Haut-Commissariat de la République Française en Allemagne, Card files of persecutees in the later French zone, Itzek Wajcman's prisoner card, Hailfingen, Nr. 40990; *The KZ-Außenlager (subcamp) at the Night-Fighter Airbase Hailfingen/Tailfingen*, pp. 38-39; Volker Mall et al, *Die Häftlinge des KZ-Außenlagers Hailfingen/Tailfingen [The prisoners of the concentration camp Hailfingen/Tailfingen]*, Herrenberg, 2020, Volume 2, p. 112. These sources, and those referenced in footnote 5 (page 54), point to a confusion in Yitzhak Weitzman's recollection that he was first in Dautmergen and then in Hailfingen. According to his prisoner cards, he arrived in Hailfingen from Stutthof on November 19, 1944, was transferred from Hailfingen to Dautmergen on February 14, 1945, and was deported from Dautmergen to Dachau on April 12, 1945.

It was a relatively small, primitive stone quarry where the only machines were the carts that carried the stones on rails. The manager, a German civilian, told us that in a moment there would be an explosion in the quarry. After the explosion we would load the stones on the carts and transfer them to the trucks or the grinding mill. He said: "You will have to transfer twenty-five full carts. After that you will get a hot drink. This task is your entrance test. We want to be sure that you are able-bodied enough to be considered productive workers."

We heard the explosion and started the backbreaking work. Then, two civilians appeared, an older man and a younger, good-looking woman. It was something unusual. We guessed that they were in the committee that would decide whether we were capable of work.

After a while, the pair went away. The guards told us that they were the owners of the quarry, a father and his daughter. Their visit was to discuss labor procedures, efficiency and output. We calmed down and went on working as best as we could. It seems that we passed the test, since they told us that we would continue to work in the quarry.

The men were exhausted and hungry. The work in the quarry was beyond our physical conditions. The discipline was as strict as in the other camps. They did not allow us to rest or talk among ourselves. The guards unleashed the dogs on anyone who "misbehaved." The food was the same as in the previous camps.

However, we soon noticed a big change in our treatment. The initiative came from the quarry's owners – especially the woman. She told the guards that she wanted to appoint a prisoner as foreman, and she chose a tall, relatively healthy prisoner for the role. Through him, she sent us a message saying that she would help us with food additions. Apparently, the guards had objected, threatening to report the irregularity to the authorities. But she disregarded the threat and placed several crates of apples near the latrines. The Jewish foreman told us to go there and help ourselves to the apples. We could not believe it. For years we had not seen or tasted any fruit. It was like a festival day for us. More than a taste of apples, it was a taste of freedom.

We had several more good days thanks to her. Even today I wonder whether she helped us because of pangs of conscience, pity, religious faith or a calculated plan to build a reputation as someone who had helped the Jews. She surely knew that the Germans were losing the war.

When the front got closer, the Germans decided to transfer us to the Dachau camp. On the day before, the Jewish foreman suddenly disappeared. There was a search but it was as if the earth had swallowed him. It soon became clear that the woman had been the brain behind the operation and that other people had helped her.

It was certainly a daring stunt. After the war, we met the Jewish foreman. He told us that she had hidden him near the quarry and that, a few days later, she took him in her car to a farther hiding place. The fact that they did not punish us in retaliation for the escape was the best evidence that the Germans were at the end of their rope. By that time, we could already hear at night the distant thunder of artillery. We knew that the end of the war was near.

# Dachau[7]

The transfer to Dachau put an end to that brief spell of "better" conditions. We were loaded into open trucks, once again wondering whether the Germans would finish us off. Many had died and those who were still alive could hardly stand on their feet.

The drive was short. The Dachau camp, which was not far from the city of Munich, had already been notorious before the war as a place where the Nazis confined and tortured political prisoners.

When we arrived, the situation was chaotic. The camp had just been hit by an air raid. Many shacks had been destroyed and burned. All over the place we saw evidence of indescribable atrocities. There was a huge pile of bodies near the gate stinking of decay. Further inside, we saw skeletal prisoners sitting around another pile. They were cutting flesh from the dead bodies and eating it.

It was a horrendous sight. We were witnessing a level of starvation and human degradation that dwarfed anything we had experienced before. Even today I feel that it is impossible to pass judgment on what those people were doing. The dead were already dead. For those who were starving, it was a way to try to stay alive.

The guards of the camp pretended to follow the rules, but it was a complete pandemonium. There was total indifference. Nobody paid attention to us. No roll call, no food, and no assignation of places in the shacks. It was sheer mayhem, hell on earth - a camp of cannibals.

---

[7] [Editor's note] Yitzhak Weizman arrived in Dachau on April 12, 1945 and was evacuated in one of the four trains that departed toward the mountains of Tyrol on April 25, 26 and 27. Sources: Arolsen Archives, Incarceration Documents, Dachau Concentration Camp, Office Cards, Itzek Wajcman's prisoner card, Nr. 156199; Volker Mall et al, *Die Häftlinge des KZ-Außenlagers Hailfingen/Tailfingen [The prisoners of the concentration camp Hailfingen/Tailfingen]*, Herrenberg, 2020, Volume 2, p. 112; Eliezer Schwartz, The Death Marches from the Dachau Camps to the Alps during the Final Days of World War II in Europe, *Dapim, Studies on the Holocaust*, Volume 25, Issue 1, 2011, p.135.

Within a few days the front lines were so close that the Germans decided to move out the prisoners that were relatively healthy and could be transferred. Drained and starved, we were loaded on stinking freight cars. Once again they were sending us to an unknown destination. We could not figure out why the Germans had not killed us. There had been enough opportunities. They still had control, since the decision to transfer us required a plan, logistics, and instructions. Our guess was that they planned to liquidate us at a time and place of their choice. Meanwhile, the train departed towards the mountains of Tyrol.

# To the mountains of Tyrol

We spent days and nights caged in the train without food. There were frequent stops to shift tracks and change locomotives. Our freight cars were dragged forward and pushed backward. Most of us were absolutely knackered and some were dying. Only later, when the ordeal was over, we found out that the last car of the convoy contained a trove of bread – the prisoners' rations for the trip, which the guards had not bothered to distribute.

The train was unable to make much progress. The railways to Tyrol had been severely damaged by the air raids. The Allies targeted our convoy, but the guards did not help us. They just left us trapped in the cars while they sought cover away from the train.

The attacks went on and on, wave after wave, almost incessantly. Locked up, exhausted, and almost dead, we thought that we would succumb to starvation or the air raids. Each minute was an eternity. We were helpless. Some of the prisoners passed out. The others were too worn out to pay them attention. Some people did not wake up again. It was a pity. We were about to be freed in a few hours, but we did not know it.

Night fell and the raids stopped. Through the night, the train cars were maneuvered endlessly. The Germans split the convoy, transferring several cars to a different track.

At dawn we heard the rumble of artillery. It got stronger and stronger until we were able to trace the shells from the moment of shooting until they hit their targets and blew up. The battlefront had caught up with us. Eventually, the train stopped in the middle of a dense forest. The tracks had been damaged. Fortunately for us, the convoy was tucked away under the canopy of the trees, invisible to the airplanes.

About an hour later we heard the cracking of light weapons. The bullets hissed above the cars. By then, the Americans must have known that it was a transport of prisoners. They aimed high to create the effect of a fight without hitting the convoy. Within minutes, American soldiers opened the doors and contemplated the atrocity in its full ugliness.

# PART III

Yitzhak Weizman

# Too weak to rejoice

We did not have strength to get out of the freight car. The moment of liberation and freedom had finally arrived, but we were in no condition to rejoice.

The soldiers helped us out of the cars and we took long, deep breaths of fresh air. A special American team was immediately assigned to take care of us. The first thing they told us was that we should not eat without supervision.

The soldiers were shocked by what they saw. We were human skeletons, sick, wounded, full of lice, filthy. It was indeed evidence of a savage atrocity, and the Americans recorded and photographed it as such. The visuals said much more than any written word.

There was a crazy stampede when the soldiers opened the last car and the moldy bread was discovered. Many fell victim to that first loaf of bread after liberation. Some died in the scramble and others as a result of overeating after years of chronic hunger.

There were doctors and paramedics in the unit that liberated us. They understood our medical condition. One of the doctors, a mature woman who had spent the war on the front with the troops, was particularly outstanding. She insisted on the danger of unsupervised eating, warning us against the consumption of animal fats or exceeding our stomach capacity.

Most of the freed prisoners ignored the warnings. They ran to the abandoned villages and collected food from the cellars, especially fats. They ate without restraint and paid a high price – painful Intestinal diseases that sometimes resulted in death.

It took us time to feel confident in our freedom. The change had been too sudden and sharp. We could not believe that it had really happened. We still looked around to see whether the German guards were following us. We wanted to stay in the place of our liberation because we were afraid of coming across German soldiers. Our prisoner garments and emaciated looks would give us up. We felt better and more secure when we were together.

The Americans stayed for a while in order to take care of us. We told them that we needed other clothes, but they refused to give us army uniforms. They said: "For the time being, you can continue wearing your striped garments. Now, they are your badges of honor. You overcame hell. Do not be ashamed or afraid. It is the Germans that should now be afraid of you."

# Revenge

Immediate after liberation we felt the urge to take revenge on the Germans. The fire of vengeance was burning in our hearts. We begged the Americans to give us the guns that they had taken from the German guards. They did not agree. We asked for other weapons but they still refused. We appealed to a high-ranking officer, explaining our wish by hand signs. He also dismissed us.

We did not give up. We found an American soldier who spoke German and he translated our request to the officer. In the end, the officer went along with it. More or less, this was what he said: "You will have some free time – a one-time opportunity to take revenge. Your striped clothes will identify you as an army of avengers. Be proud of them. We cannot give you guns, but you may find a crate of hand grenades in the field. Go to the nearest village and throw the grenades without pangs of conscience. We will supervise you from some distance."

Some soldiers showed us how to use the grenades. It was difficult for us to hold down the spring after we pulled out the safety-catch. The weakest were not allowed to participate in the operation.

The officer said that we had to come back to the same place in the forest. Everything was improvised and hurried. We had to take advantage of the chaotic first hours of liberation before the arrival of the regular occupation forces.

We ran like lunatics until we reached the outskirts of the nearest village. We saw a big cowshed and other structures with roofs covered with green grass, as was very common in Germany and Poland. We threw the grenades into the cowshed. In a matter of minutes the fire spread to the other structures. The flames reminded us of the Birkenau crematoriums, where month after month the fires went up crying to heaven. There was big damage to property and animals, but we never knew if anyone was killed or wounded. The name of the village was Stallham.

We ran back to our starting point in the forest with a feeling of enormous satisfaction. It was a small retaliation, but we had taken revenge on the cursed criminals who had tortured and abused us for years. Some of us wanted to join the American army and fight. Of course, it was impossible to fulfill that wish.

In those first hours and days, the American soldiers wanted to give us everything they had. We compulsively hoarded food. They told us again and again that hoarding food was no longer necessary, but it was to no avail. We could not stop doing it.

Eventually, the Americans continued their advance. They left behind a small team, mostly medical personnel, to take care of us. Many of us were sick. I suffered from intestinal disorders, probably dysentery. But I did not need the infusions that were administered to many of the others. The pain passed and I recovered within a couple of days.

We spent the first night after liberation in the forest, near the convoy's freight cars. They gave us mattresses and blankets and we enjoyed a warm bed in the free open air. The next day we woke up confused. We could not get used to the idea that we were truly free.

After sobering up from the drunkenness of freedom, we faced problems for which we did not have clear answers. We had survived, but what should we do? Where should we go? Who wanted us?

On that day, I felt that for the first time in my life I had to make choices about my destiny. For the time being, I decided to stay with the group of liberated prisoners that were transferred to the city of Landsberg.

# Landsberg

We were housed in the huge buildings of a former base of the Wehrmacht. Many liberated prisoners were in Landsberg waiting for what was coming next. Returning to Poland was a choice that I would not consider. I swore that I would never go back to Poland. For me it was a huge cemetery, a cursed land. If anyone from my family was still alive I would find out sooner or later.

Staying in Germany and waiting for a visa to the United States was a possibility. I also remembered that I had an aunt and uncle in Paris. Had they survived the war? Perhaps I should go to France.

Most enticing was the possibility of going to the Eretz Israel. I had dreamed about it since I was a boy in the youth movement Hashomer Hatzair in Gombin. But that alternative seemed the least realistic. Palestine was still under British rule, and the mandatory authorities were not allowing the immigration of survivors.

I had to decide for better or worse. It could not be avoided. I had to come to terms with the consequences of the war. I was all alone, without family. Nobody could give me advice or provide help. I was physically weak and did not have any money.

The Landsberg compound was partly destroyed, big and grey. There were lots of people who spoke many different languages - liberated prisoners from Russia, Ukraine, France, Poland and other former German occupied countries. Many of them were women who had been brought to Germany as slave workers and were now trying to go back home. But the biggest group were those who had been liberated from the concentration and forced labor camps.

Some people met relatives that they thought were dead, but such cases were rare. Like other DP (displaced persons) camps, Landsberg was open - we were free to come and go. The conditions were of course much better than in the German camps, but it was still a camp.

After some time we got used to freedom and overcame our fears. We started to go out to town and to neighboring villages. We saw Germans living quiet lives. In the villages the men were watering their fields and the farms were blooming. The thought that most of those men had probably been in the army, faithfully serving the Nazis, was infuriating. We could not accept that they were returning to life as usual while the lives of the survivors of their crimes had been reduced to ruins and orphanhood. In the DP camps, people were bitter and angry. We still wanted revenge.

A group of former prisoners, me included, decided to form a commando unit to hunt for SS men. It was a spontaneous thing. We went out wearing the striped hats from the camps and the Star of David patches on our chests. Our intention was to catch them and hand them over to the American authorities to stand trial.

Without anyone's permission we broke into houses claiming that we knew that SS men were hiding there. We indiscriminately grabbed men under the age of sixty and brought them to the Americans, saying that they were former soldiers gone underground.

I must say that those were dark times in the twilight of war. One could still smell the fires and the dead bodies. There was fear and uncertainly. In times like that, people like us behaved as if law and order did not exist and life was cheap.

The Germans were scared of us. They knew that we wanted revenge. Most of them did not resist arrest. We led them through the streets of Landsberg with satisfaction and glee. We waved our sticks yelling and kicking. Somehow, we felt vindicated by the privilege of parading humiliated and frightened Germans in Germany

We wished we had weapons. Who knows what we would have done if we were armed. The Americans forbade us to continue our searches. We had to stop.

The days passed in idleness and without worries. My physical recovery was quick. I gained weight, changed my clothes and looked better, but I was still very thin.

Most of the Jews in the Landsberg DP camp wanted to go to Palestine, but the Americans ignored that. When we began organizing protest demonstrations they passed on our demand to the authorities that dealt with the refugees. Their response was that the chances of going to Palestine were slim because the British had set a very low monthly limit for immigration visas.

In the meantime, lots of people were leaving the DP camp every day. The Russians, the French, the Poles, and the Dutch were returning to their countries. We acutely felt the homelessness of the Jews. I was troubled by the fact that I was free but still in a camp.

Some of my liberated friends from Gombin were going to the United States, including Lajzer Bocian, Mendel Wrobel and Zalman Tatarka. But I was more convinced than ever that the only place for me was Eretz Israel.

One day, like angels from heaven, a group of soldiers wearing a Star of David set on vertical stripes of blue and white came to visit the camp. Our excitement and joy had no limits. For the first time in our lives we saw Jewish soldiers carrying weapons. They were part of the Jewish Brigade of the British army, which was made up of Jews from Palestine commanded by Anglo-Jewish officers (they called Palestine by its Hebrew name – Eretz Israel, the same name that we used in Gombin), We could not believe our eyes. We were so proud of them! Just seeing them strengthened in me the wish to go to Eretz Israel. They awakened in me again all my latent dreams that suddenly became true. In my worst days of suffering, I had dreamt about seeing upright Jews, proud and carrying weapons.

The unit of the Jewish Brigade started to organize a route to take us out of the Landsberg DP camp and prepare us to go to Eretz Israel legally or illegally. Their first priority was the youth. After a few days, the Jewish Brigade soldiers quietly told us to be ready to leave on short notice. They did not disclose our destination. They simply said that we had to maintain secrecy, stay in the camp and wait for further instructions.

We did not have to wait long. That same night they organized us in groups and took us from the town center to the suburbs. A convoy of Jewish Brigade trucks was waiting for us. The drivers spoke Hebrew. The trucks were numbered. Each group knew to which truck they been assigned.

Everything was done at maximum speed. The operation took a very short time. The convoy darted through the night towards the Italian border. The trucks were covered with tarpaulin. Most of us slept. We felt secure in the hands of the Jewish Brigade.

After a long drive we stopped for a while. They told us to stay in the truck and maintain silence. We continued for a while and stopped again. Then they told us that we had crossed the Italian border - we could come out and even sing.

My friends Lajzer Bocian, Mendel Wrobel and Zalman Tatarka. Like me, they were in DP camps in Germany before emigrating to the US.

Landsberg DP camp for Jewish refugees. Image source: United States Holocaust Memorial Museum.

In Landsberg, refugees protest against British immigration restrictions to Palestine. Image source: Yad Vashem.

Jewish Brigade soldiers smuggling refugees from the DP camps in Germany. The refugees were taken to Italian camps where they waited for a place in one of the illegal immigrant ships that sailed to Palestine. Image source: United States Holocaust Memorial Museum.

# Italy

The year was 1945, several weeks after the end of the war in Europe. The Jewish Brigade had succeeded in bringing us to Italy. We had arrived at the right check post, found the right guards, and crossed the border according to plan. In Italy, the Jewish Brigade operated more freely and with more means than in any other country. Italy was their main base - the country where they had fought during the war.

After a short rest, we went on driving until we arrived at a small village in the south. It was a fishermen's village on the beach called Santa Maria. A poor, barely populated place. Some of the houses were in ruins. There were no greeneries or trees in the village.

The DP camp was located in the outskirts. We settled in a building that was used by the Jewish Brigade as living quarters and school. There, we started our new life. We had a chance to study and complete part of the education that we had missed during the war. In a very short time the Brigade soldiers managed to set up a program based on the curriculum of the Eretz Israeli schools. All the lessons were in Hebrew. Our wish to learn was very strong. We had been isolated from the world and we had lost our best school years.

I put care and effort in my studies. Most of us stopped speaking Yiddish or Polish on principle – we only wanted to speak Hebrew. A library with books from Eretz Israel was our main source for information and knowledge. We used it very often.

We were very interested in learning about Eretz Israel and the Yishuv (the Hebrew word for the Jewish community in Palestine). We had suffered enough in the diaspora and it was obvious to us that our place was in the future Jewish state.

Our schedule included sports, fitness training, and self-defense lessons. It was like a pre-military program. We were still very thin and had lost muscular strength. The exercises were effective in speeding up our physical recovery.

I remember our time in Santa Maria not only as a period of physical rehabilitation but also as a time of spiritual, intellectual and mental renewal. My whole way of thinking changed. Fright and worry had been at the core of my existence through the war years. Now, I

74

did not have to worry about basic survival and could free myself from the prisoner's mentality. I made an effort to shut off the past as much as possible. Of course, I longed for my family, especially my parents and sister. As a free person, I felt their absence all the more. I still thought that I might meet them some day, although deep in my heart I knew that it was a hopeless dream.

The time in Santa Maria prepared me for a normal life. I felt more self-confident made progress in my studies. The belief in the future was sustained by a goal that I was eager to fulfill. We all knew that, sooner or later, our turn to go to Eretz Israel would come.

Among those preparing for aliyah ("going up" – the Hebrew word for going to Eretz Israel), we had first priority. We were teenagers, boys and girls who were nearly old enough to serve in the Hagana - the military organization of the Yishuv that would later become Israel's army.

In Santa Maria, the study-groups were organized by political affiliation. I chose to join the group of Hashomer Hatzair, the youth movement to which I had belonged in Gombin.

It was the end of 1945 and the Jewish Brigade was at the peak of its efforts to smuggle survivors from the Italian DP camps to Eretz Israel. The economic situation in Italy was miserable. Poverty and hunger were rampant. People roamed the streets asking for a piece of bread. The Italians knew that we received assistance from Jewish organizations and that our situation was much better than theirs. Some of them came to Santa Maria hoping to get help from the Brigade soldiers or the Jewish refugees.

Italy had been chosen as a departure zone for the illegal aliyah because of its geographical location, its many harbors, and the fact that the Jewish units of the British army were based there. Since the Italian government never made a formal decision to allow the passage of refugees through the country, the entire effort relied on clandestine activities.

In that context, the fact that the Italian government chose to overlook the illegal nature of what the Jews were doing was a huge help. The other important factor was the favorable attitude of the population. Rather than hostile or angry, the Italian people were sympathetic and cooperative. Without all that help it would have been impossible to bring into Italy those large numbers of European Jewish refugees and surreptitiously send them to Eretz Israel.

Santa Maria al Bagno, home to the largest DP camp in southern Italy. Image source: Museo della Memoria e dell'Accoglienza.

At the seashore near Santa Maria. I am standing in the middle.

With a bicycle in Santa Maria's harbor quayside.

Soccer team of Santa Maria Jewish refugees. I am the fourth standing player from left.

Santa Maria al Bagno's Museum of Memory and Hospitality, focused on the Jewish refugees' sojourn in the town and the solidarity of the local community. Image source: Museo della Memoria e dell'Accoglienza.

# Quotas

After more than a year of studies and impatient waiting, we finally got the message to prepare for our illegal aliyah. Two days later a Brigade envoy gave us good and bad news. On that same night we would leave to a rendezvous place and continue to the port of departure, but only thirty of us would have clearance to go. That was our group's quota for that departure. The meaning of it was that the group would have to be divided. Some would sail to Eretz Israel and others would be left behind.

It was a thorny situation. We gathered with the teachers to make a decision. Should we split the group or wait for an opportunity to go together? It was impossible to know how long we would have to wait for the next available ship. We had planned to build together a new collective life in Eretz Israel. Splitting the group could mean the beginning of its disintegration. The discussion was strained and stormy. The majority thought that we should take the opportunity, even if it meant splitting the group.

We cast lots to determine who would go that night. Since my name was not drawn, I did not sail with that first group. Their ship succeeded in evading the British blockade and reaching Eretz Israel. Upon arrival, they went to Kibbutz Mizra, where they immediately began to study and work. We corresponded with them during the rest of our stay in Santa Maria. Their letters and stories about the warm welcome they received encouraged us. Now we had first-hand information about Eretz Israel and the way of life in the kibbutz.

The urge to go to Eretz Israel grew stronger. We staged peaceful demonstrations in the cities near Santa Maria to denounce the British restrictions to the entry of Jewish refugees to Eretz Israel. The Italian citizens showed sympathy. The stream of refugees from Germany to Italy gained strength and there was international pressure on the British to raise the quotas of entry permits to Palestine. The British government, however, did not bend to the pressure.

We went back to the routine of our studies. We learned Hebrew and continued our physical recovery. Many of us, including me, added height and weight to the point of reaching normal dimensions.

I loved studying, but I was also enthusiastic about playing soccer. We formed a team of Santa Maria Jewish refugees that turned out to be quite competitive. I remember a particular match against the team of one of the neighboring towns. When we won the game, their fans threw stones at us. The crowd behaved wildly, shouting anti-Semitic slurs. At one point, they seemed ready to tear us apart. We managed to extricate ourselves and reach the truck that waited for us near the field. That night there were rumors that the fans would come to Santa Maria to attack us. We assembled on the upper floor, collected sticks and stones, and prepared for the battle. Fortunately, they did not show up.

The incident revealed a latent streak of anti-Semitism among the Italians. But we did not back off. We continued to play against Italian teams, often surprising them with our skills. Sometimes we were ourselves dazzled by our successes.

We learned to have fluent conversations In Hebrew, strictly maintaining our resolution to avoid Yiddish and Polish. It was not easy. We scolded each other when someone failed. That determination proved to be effective in helping us overcome the difficulties of learning a new language.

The teachers continued to instruct us about life of Eretz Israel. The dedicated work of the soldiers of the Jewish Brigade inspired us. We were ready and happy to perform any task that they asked us to undertake.

Our life became a permanent demonstration. Every day we arranged ourselves in rows holding signs and slogans against the British in the dining-hall. Reporters came often to take photographs that were published in newspapers for the world to see. That period was full of meaning, at least for me. I learned to see and understand things in a more mature way.

# July 1946

All good things eventually end, and that was also true for the wonderful time we spent in Italy. In late July, we received an order to be ready to move within the next few hours. We packed in a hurry our few belongings. Happy, excited and impatient we waited for confirmation, hoping that it would not be a false alarm.

This time we were not disappointed. We left at night in covered British trucks escorted by soldiers of the Jewish Brigade. After a long drive we arrived to a rendezvous point near our port of departure.

We knew that we would stay there for a short time. Our group was taken to a secluded house where they explained to us that we would receive a course to prepare us for a special role on the ship.

During the two-day course they gave guidance to replace the Italian team if the British discovered the ship (if that happened, the Italian team would mix in with the passengers). They also prepared us to provide assistance to the Italian and Eretz Israeli teams from the moment of sailing. We learned that that there were going to be many logistical, organizational and social problems on the ship.

The Eretz Israeli team made us feel that the success of the operation depended on us. We were proud that they had chosen us for that role. The ship in which we were about to sail was anchored off the coast. All the equipment, food and medicines had to be ferried by small motorboats before the passengers boarded. We worked through the night loading the boats and transferring the cargo to the ship. Divided into small units, we then joined the motorboats to help the old and the sick. The sea was restless and the boats were overloaded because we had to transfer all the passengers before daybreak. More than once we were in danger of capsizing. Doing that job was a thrilling experience.

When we first approached it at night, the ship looked huge. When day broke, however, we saw its real size. It was a nutshell of a ship - old, dirty and rusty. It was a small freighter for merchandise and animals, not intended for people. The original loading fixtures had been removed and replaced with wooden planks that resembled the bunks where we slept in the camps.

The overcrowding was awful. Moving among the planks was almost impossible. After transferring and placing the passengers, we had to take care of organizing things and maintain order in the ship. Everyone had to stay inside. Being on the deck was forbidden during the day and restricted at night. People were lying like sardines in a can. There were 790 passengers on the ship – far exceeding the weight that the vessel was supposed to carry. From the first moment, we knew that we were facing a safety and organization nightmare.

The ship's name was Kaf Gimel Yordei Hasira, which roughly translates as The Twenty-three Seamen who Went Down (Kaf Gimel stands for the number 23 in the Hebrew system of lettered numbers). The name had been chosen to memorialize the twenty-three Palmach commandos who had disappeared in 1941 while on a secret seaborne mission to sabotage oil refineries in Tripoli (during the Second World War, the Palmach commandos of the Hagana participated in joint operations with the British against Vichy France targets in Lebanon and Syria).

*Yitzhak Weizman*

# PART IV

# The sailing[8]

The Kaf Gimel sailed on August 2nd 1946, one day after the departure of the ship Katriel Yaffe (the name of the commander of the twenty-three disappeared Palmach commandos), and from the same port of Metaponto. Most people on board were from Poland. The commander was Israel Aharonov (later Oren), assisted by Israel Rozenblum (later Rotem) and Yitzhak Etkin as wireless radio operator.

According to the original plan we had to transfer part of the passengers and the teams (except the Italian team) to the deck of Katriel Yaffe in the middle of the sea. Because of engine trouble our boat sailed very slowly with the help of a sail. We were unable to meet the other ship and faced unexpected problems resulting from the lack of food, water, and medicines to treat the sick. All the plans went wrong.

As an organized group, we had to maintain order, encourage people, and give help to those who needed it. As I said, we were also supposed to replace the Italian team in case of trouble. It was not a simple job. Among the passengers, there were pregnant women and

---

[8] [Editor's note] While Yitzhak Weizman writes that the ships Katriel Yaffe and Kaf Gimel sailed from Metaponto, all the sources, including documents about illegal aliyah ships and testimonies of other passengers, indicate that their point of departure was Bocca di Magra near La Spezia. It appears, then, that this is another case in which the author confused elements from two different memories. In this particular instance, he seems to be mixing the recollection of his own sailing on the Kaf Gimel with another memory about a different illegal aliyah ship that departed from Metaponto. A possible candidate would be the ship Shabtai Lozinski, which left Metaponto on March 4, 1947 and, after eluding the British blockade, went aground on the shore of Palestine near Nitzanim on March 13. The arrival of the Shabtai Lozinski caused a big stir in the Yishuv. Thousands of Jewish residents flocked to the site in order to mix with the refugees, create confusion, and try to prevent their capture by the British. The incidents must have made a deep impression on Yitzhak Weizman, who had just arrived in Palestine a few weeks before. Sources: Daniel Rosenne, *Gideonim, Wireless Operators in the Service of an Emerging State*, Association for the Commemoration of the Fallen Soldiers of the IDF Signal Corps, 2018, pp. 180-183; Palestine Immigration Website, *The story of the sailing of the Kaf Gimel* (http://www.palyam.org/Hahapala/Teur_haflagot/hf_KG_Yordei_Hasira.php); Palestine Immigration Website, *The Voyage of the Shabtai Luzinski* (http://www.palyam.org/English/Hahapala/hf/hf_Shabtai_Luzinski.pdf).

other people who did not stop vomiting. The truth was that we ourselves did not feel well. We were terribly tired and worried about the condition of the ship, which was not disclosed to the passengers to avoid panic.

A week passed and we were making minimal progress. The commander instructed us to reduce the rations of food and water. Things got worse when the ship began to lean on one side. There was a crack in the hull and water was seeping into one of the holds. The emergency pumps were activated but their capacity was low. Few people on the ship knew about it, but after a day or two the passengers began to notice that something was happening. The nervousness grew, tension mounted and panic started. We could not hide the fact that the ship was taking water. Disobeying instructions, the passengers started to come up to the deck. We were beginning to lose control. Had the passengers been aware of the real extent of the damage, the situation would had become unmanageable. In that desperate situation, we had to calm the passengers and lie, telling them that they should not worry.

The Italian captain was unable to contact the ship Katriel Yaffe or the ports in the area. Our life was again in danger. It never occurred to us that so soon after our liberation from the Nazi hell, we would face death again. The context, of course, was very different. Now we had a cause – we were on our way to start a new life in Eretz Israel. But once again we confronted the question: what was the purpose of fighting for life when the cost was life itself?

I had no doubt that I had made the right choice. Since my childhood, I had suffered and been humiliated because I was a Jew. It was the first, and perhaps the last chance to fulfill the dream of going to Eretz Israel. For my parents, it would have been difficult to understand that dream. Many Polish Jews had emigrated to Eretz Israel before the war. My family certainly had the financial means to do the same, but they never saw it as a necessity or something they wanted to do.

I did not lose the hope that despite of all the troubles we would reach our goal. But there were almost 800 passengers on the ship and a few people began to act irrationally. Fortunately, the majority withstood the pressure and behaved wisely. Some of them actually helped us organize activities, singing and games to distract the crowd from worry and fear.

After two weeks at sea we were standing on the deck waiting for a miracle and, like in a fairy tale, it eventually happened. A reconnaissance British airplane appeared on the horizon and approached our ship. It made rounds above us before disappearing. The British had spotted us. We did not know whether to be happy or sad. We knew that they would rescue us, but it was very unlikely that they would allow us to enter Palestine.

Within a few hours, we saw a large warship coming towards us. The British boarded our ship, tied it to theirs, and towed us to the port of Haifa. On August 15th 1946 I reached Eretz Israel for the first time, but not as I had expected. I did not have the privilege of entering it. We just stayed in the harbor.

The Katriel Jaffe, which had also been intercepted by the British, had arrived at Haifa on the previous day. At the port, British soldiers armed with clubs and guns transferred the refugees of both boats to a deportation ship. Despite our exhaustion, we managed to resist for several hours.

The British soldiers used reasonable force. They overcame us using tear-gas and water jets. But nobody was taken to the deportation ship without resistance. The British dragged us one by one. Some wanted to jump out and swim to the shore, but they were deterred by rumors that the British had placed mines around the ship.

The name of the deportation ship was Empire Heywood. When the British completed our transfer it sailed to Famagusta. Within twenty-four hours we were again in a camp, this time in Cyprus.

The illegal immigrants' ship Kaf Gimel Yordei Hasira, being towed into Haifa harbor by the British destroyer HMS Brissenden. Image source: Palmach Museum.

Posters calling for a protest rally against the deportations to Cyprus. Image source: Israel National Photo Collection.

Deported illegal immigrants registering in a British detainee camp in Cyprus. Image source: Ghetto Fighters House Archives.

Palmach fighters' escape tunnel in Cyprus. Image source: Israel National Photo Collection.

Panoramic view of British detainee camp in Cyprus. Image source: Ghetto Fighters House Archives.

Detainees' protest in Cyprus Image source: Ghetto Fighters House Archives.

# Cyprus

In Cyprus, they took us to Camp 60, the first of a line of camps near the seashore. The Italian team and the Eretz Israeli team, including our Palmach escorts, were also transferred with us.

During the first few days we were instructed to approach the fence in the evening and stay there monitoring the British guards on the lookout towers. Night after night we watched them while the Palmach fighters dug a tunnel to escape. They had agents outside the camp who organized their clandestine return to Eretz Israel. Being in the watch group was a big responsibility - we had to take an oath of secrecy, swearing that we would not talk if caught.

The oath taking ceremony was a very solemn affair. One by one we entered a dark tent and stood in front of the commander. There was a pistol and a Bible on the table. We laid one hand on the pistol and the other hand on the Bible. The commander whispered the words and we repeated: "I swear my allegiance to the Hagana, my commitment to secrecy, and my readiness to perform any task with dedication and self-sacrifice." We were transfixed by the ceremony. We felt that we were taking part in the struggle against the British.

Camp 60 got bigger and bigger because most of the ships were caught. Just days before our arrival in Haifa, the British had announced that all illegal immigrants would be deported to Cyprus. We had been among the first deportees. Once again, we were surrounded by barbed-wire fences and locked under guard. We were very close to Eretz Israel, but getting there was a distant prospect.

Fortunately, we did not succumb to depression. The youth guides from Eretz Israel took care of us, organizing a daily schedule of studies, sports, and social activities. Staying active was the best way to avoid sliding back to the prisoners' mentality.

During that time in Cyprus our group took its first steps towards communal life. The group's name was Geulim (Hebrew word for "redeemed") because we had been saved from the Nazi hell. We ran a communal kitchen and put whatever money we had in a collective fund. We appointed a secretary, a treasurer and a committee of social and cultural activities. The comradeship gave us confidence and reinforced our shared interests. Groups like ours were exceptional in the camp. Many outsiders wanted to join us but we refrained from taking in new people who were unknown to us.

We continued to study and speak Hebrew among ourselves. We received letters from our friends in Mizra and our guides kept us informed about events in Eretz Israel. Our living conditions in Cyprus were not very comfortable. Compared to the German camps, however, Camp 60 was a paradise. We were not free but we had everything we needed and the British did not interfere in our life. We could do anything we wanted and had plenty of free time. Being part of an organized group enabled us to use that time in healthy, productive ways.

I also had the privilege of visiting the town of Famagusta, which was not far from the camp. Since I was in charge of the group's supplies, I went there with one of our youth guides from Eretz Israel to do the shopping. The British allowed it as a one-time exception. On another occasion, I strained a muscle playing soccer and went to receive treatment at Famagusta's hospital. I stayed there for almost a week, enjoying the clean white bed and the attention of kind-hearted nurses. It was a reinvigorating time in an atmosphere of freedom and warmth.

After that nice experience, I returned to the less comfortable conditions of the camp. As I have said, those conditions were tolerable for us. We did not suffer physical or material deprivation and, to be honest, the British treated us in a way that was relatively fair and considerate. Our grievances with them were more political than anything else. We were angry with the British because they had locked the gates to Eretz Israel. For us, they were the main political enemy.

We followed closely the news from Mandatory Palestine. We knew that in the Jewish Yishuv people were furious about the British deportation of the refugees. There were angry protests and the British had to impose a curfew in Haifa. Here are a couple of quotes from the newspapers we received at the time:

> *"During the night the British army hunted curfew breakers who wanted to replenish food supplies. They locked up to 1,500 people in two big plots, one near Shell and the other in Shukery street. In the morning of August 13th 1946, when the intention to deport illegal Jewish immigrants was announced, thousands broke the curfew and marched*

*towards the port. The community council declared a general strike. Many people gathered in Kiryat Eliyahu and Hadar Hacarmel. In Zvulun street, the British soldiers shot and killed three protestors: Avigail Weinbrand (age 19), Emil Malitz (age 30) and Zeev Carmy (age 14). Those were the first victims of the campaign against the deportations to Cyprus. In the course of the day, seven additional demonstrators were wounded. Evening protest meetings were held in the National Fund's Square in Hadar Hacarmel."*

*"The ship Katriel Jaffe was discovered not far from Haifa. When it reached the harbor it tried to slip away by sabotaging the anchor's chain, accompanied by loud singing of the passengers. The wind pushed the ship towards Kiryat Hayim, but an Arab policemen noticed it and the ship was chained to the coast cruiser HMS Mauritius that carried 1,500 soldiers. The ship commander was ordered to let the soldiers board the ship without resistance, but to oppose any attempt to transfer the passengers to the deportation ship to Cyprus. Explosives were smuggled aboard the ship in order to damage the deportation ship Empire Highwood. The passengers fiercely resisted the transfer. First they hid in the ship's holds. The men stood arm-in-arm surrounding the women and facing the water jets that the British soldiers splashed on them. The soldiers did not use firearms – they overcame the passengers with clubs and tear gas. In order to prevent the passengers from jumping into the sea the soldiers laid depth sea mines around the ship. Palmach warriors from the unit of marine sabotage succeeded to sneak into the lower hold of the ship and put the explosives there. There was an explosion, but it did not cause much damage. Still, the sailing of the Empire Highwood was delayed for four days. Only then were the passengers deported to Cyprus."*.

We were heartened by the support of the Yishuv. We felt that we were already an organic part of a community that cared and did not forget us. Knowing that we were not alone, we also organized protest actions in Camp 60, hoping that the struggle would force the hand of the British.

On New Year Eve 1947, after four months in Cyprus, we received the good news that we would be allowed to enter Eretz Israel. The messengers told us to be ready to leave within one or two days. We could not avoid being skeptical - we had long experience with false rumors. But more ships of illegal immigrants had been coming, the protests in the Yishuv and in the Cyprus camps had impact, and the British were facing a lot of international pressure to open the gates to the Jewish refugees. In the end, they modified their policy. The deportations would continue, but they increased the quota of entry permits for Holocaust survivors. Since we had been among the first deported to Cyprus, we were among the first to benefit from the additional permits.

Confirming that the good news was not a false rumor, an envoy of the Jewish Agency brought the forms with the names of those who had permission to enter Eretz Israel.

Our joy knew no boundaries. We cried, hugged, and kissed like dreamers whose fantasies came true. We dismantled the tents and quickly packed our meager personal belongings and everything we had in our common store - food, clothes, footgear and books. We knew that we would need all those things for continuing our communal way of life in Eretz Israel.

Those were hours of elation. Our feeling of victory and freedom exceeded what we had experienced when we were liberated from the Nazis. Back then, we did not know where we were going. We felt like the wandering Jew - without a place on earth that we could call our homeland.  Now the situation was very different. We had been preparing to go to Eretz Israel for a long time and we had attained our goal. We had taken risks for that happy moment. We had confronted the dangers of illegal immigration into Eretz Israel. And we had done it all without the slightest hesitation.

We organized a farewell party inviting our guides and other people from the camp. It was an evening of happiness celebrating that we were finally leaving the camps behind and starting a normal free life. Still, we suspected that the realities of Eretz Israel would not be as rosy as we imagined.

# Apprehensions and doubts

We had a general idea of what was going on in Eretz Israel and in the kibbutzim. The struggle of the Yishuv was taking a big toll in terms of arrests, casualties and victims. We knew that it was not by chance that young people like us were given priority as immigrants. The Yishuv needed us. There was an ongoing fight against the British and a clear sense that it would be followed by a bitter war with the Arab countries. It was very likely that we would have to join the battle for Eretz Israel without completing our studies.

The dream was becoming reality, but practical thinking was necessary in order to avoid false illusions and disappointments. Fortunately, we had enough experience with hardships and with drastic changes in locations and living conditions. We believed that we would be able to adjust to our life in Eretz Israel without too many difficulties and crises.

Still, we had apprehensions about the comrades who were already in Kibbutz Mizra. Would we succeed in restoring our ties and functioning again as one group? It was logical to expect that the long separation and our disparate experiences had shaped differences in the mentalities of the two parts of the group. It was going to be difficult to bridge the gap. We had been corresponding after they left Italy, but only a few of the people of the Mizra group had been involved in those exchanges and, with the passage of time, we had been receiving less and less letters from them.

Most of us were convinced that our place was in the kibbutz. With very few exceptions, we were orphans – youngsters who had lost their parents and families and were alone in the world. Since nobody else was waiting for us in Eretz Israel, we hoped that the comrades who had arrived before us had laid the ground for our reception and integration as part of the kibbutz community.

However, many things had changed in two years. The first group had been successfully absorbed in Mizra. They studied, worked and received military training in the Palmach. They had merged with another youth group whose members were not known to us. There was mutual satisfaction between them and the founders of the kibbutz. They had good relations with the young people and some of them had married with daughters and sons of the founders. In short, the group had changed mentally and socially as part of their adjustment to life in the kibbutz and in Eretz Israel.

We still wanted to go to Mizra, but we were troubled by the fact that the recent correspondence from the first group had been scanty and unenthusiastic. We could not avoid the feeling that they had been losing interest in our reunion.

Then, just a few hours before we left the Cyprus camp, someone from Hashomer Hatzair told us that we should not entertain the illusion that Kibbutz Mizra would take us in. The maximum that Hashomer Hatzair could say, but not promise, was that they would try to place us in another kibbutz near Mizra.

For me, this was very disappointing. As one of the most devoted members and organizers of the group, I had been strongly committed to the vision of a future life together in the kibbutz. Some of my comrades said that, even if we were allowed to join Mizra, we should not go there. They felt offended by the lack of interest of the first group and they thought that we should not grovel. Others said that we could not blame the whole group for the indifference of some leaders. In the end, we agreed that we would not make any decisions until we got more clarity about the situation in Eretz Israel.

Tense and impatient we sat on our packages and crates. After a nerve-wrecking wait, the British trucks arrived and took us to Famagusta. There was a ship at the port that would take us to Eretz Israel. As we approached, we felt uncomfortable that the British solders still kept us under heavy guard. When they refused to allow us to move freely around the port and do some shopping we asked why they were still treating us as prisoners. Their response was: "Those were the orders that we received. For us, you are still prisoners." We felt angry and depressed. Suddenly, we were overwhelmed by the suspicion that the whole thing was a trick of the British. Could it be that they were transferring us to a different place, farther away from Eretz Israel?

Our bitter experiences had taught us to be wary, especially in a context in which the Yishuv was rebelling and the British were harshly repressing the protest demonstrations in Eretz Israel. In the end, we boarded the ship with mixed feelings. We walked along the pier by a line of soldiers and stood in front of the boarding plank. We were somber, thinking our own thoughts and waiting to see what the British had in store for us.

Our camp guides came to bid us farewell. They tried to cheer us up with songs and conversation, but we were not in a mood to respond. When they learned about our suspicions, one of them approached the British senior officer and asked him to reassure us that we were sailing to Eretz Israel. The officer came to us and said: "We have orders to be strict with you, but British soldiers are fair and they are not liars. You can be at ease about your destination." When we heard that, we started cheering, dancing and singing in front of the astonished British soldiers. We were so joyful that we did not feel the passing of time until we saw the outline of Mount Carmel and the dancing lights of the city of Haifa. It was a wonderful sight.

# Eretz Israel

As we approached the shore the blaze of the lights expanded and the neighborhoods of Haifa could be seen in their entire splendor. We were proud to see a Jewish city bustling with life. The dream was coming true.

We crowded on the deck as the ship maneuvered into the port. Four people in a small motorboat approached us waving their hands. Using an amplifier, they asked if there were passengers who did not feel well or were seriously sick. I will always remember this because the expression "seriously sick" reminded me of the Germans' selections. But we were in Eretz Israel, they repeated the question in Hebrew, and in that context the implications of "being sick" were totally different.

The date was January 1, 1947. The ship cast anchor in the harbor. We had really arrived. We expected to disembark free and happy, but the British thought otherwise. We were still under guard and had to obey their instructions. We did not understand what was going on. Why did we have to climb on trucks accompanied by British guards? Where were the Jewish Agency people? Did they know about our arrival? And where were our friends from Mizra, who should have been there welcoming us?

Later we heard that the British had closed the port and were not allowing the presence of civilians, especially Jews. Under the custody of four British guards we left the port in a tarpaulin-covered truck. We had mixed feelings - happy to be in Eretz Israel, but angry that the British were not releasing us. We did not know where they were taking us. The guards were courteous and polite. They told us that the drive would be short and that we were going to Atlit - a camp for detained illegal immigrants.

We were shocked. We had entry permits from the British. Why were they taking us to a detainee camp? The guards explained the situation. We would be in Atlit until the Mandatory authorities formally admitted us according to the quota of permits. Meanwhile, all the admissions were suspended as retaliation for the Yishuv's protests against the deportations to Cyprus.

We arrived at the Atlit camp. It was a real prisoners' camp with fences and watchtowers with armed soldiers. The sight reminded us of the not so distant past. We felt frustrated, but there was no choice – we had to accept the situation. We were comforted by the fact that at least we were in Eretz Israel and the British were saying that our stay in the camp would be temporary.

In Atlit we met hundreds of people from many different countries. They had been there for weeks and in some cases for months. There were few families with children. Most of the detainees were alone and the atmosphere was gloomy. Just the fact that we, Holocaust survivors, were imprisoned in a crowded camp brought us back to the days that we wanted to forget.

In the camp we were free to do whatever we wanted, but we did not organize our group for a long-term stay. We received hints that we would be freed soon. Guides from the youth movements came regularly to organize social activities and keep us informed.

We thought that someone from the group in Mizra would come to visit, but they did not show up. The truth was that we were not too interested in meeting with them. We understood that the bond between the two groups had been severed.

The days passed slowly. It was rainy and cold. The mud and dirt contributed to our bad mood. The days seemed to stretch forever because of the boredom. Personally, I was troubled by the fact that a year and a half had passed since the end of the war, and I had not had an opportunity to search for members of my extended family. Just as it was almost unbelievable that I had survived, it might be that someone else had survived too.

In the Atlit camp the thoughts about loneliness started bothering me again. I remembered that I had an aunt, my father's sister, who lived in France before the war. Her married family name was Glowinski. I also remembered that my father's brother Leon had emigrated to South America, but I could not recall whether he had gone to Argentina or Chile. I tried in my imagination to construct a jigsaw puzzle of the family members dispersed in different parts of the world.

The thoughts about my immediate family and more distant relatives brought me back to the days of my happy childhood. I dreamed that I was meeting members of my family and we were talking about my childhood memories. Then I would wake up in the morning to the gray, depressing reality of the camp. When I told my friends about my recurring dreams, I discovered that I was not the only one. Many survivors had similar dreams for quite a long period.

They told us several times that our release was near. We began to doubt it because there were many people in the camp who had arrived before us and were still there. On the other hand, it was true that, unlike us, they were not part of an organized group sponsored by a political organization.

Thanks to the efforts of the Jewish Agency, the Youth Aliyah organization (Aliyat Hanoar in Hebrew) and the Hashomer Hatzair kibbutz movement, we were released after several weeks and transferred to a transition camp of the Jewish Agency in Kiryat Shmuel.

The Atlit camp, where illegal immigrants were kept in administrative detention. Image source: Wikimedia Commons.

A group of illegal immigrants arriving at the Atlit camp. Image source: Israel National Photo Collection

Kiryat Shmuel, near Haifa, was the first immigrant camp of the Jewish Agency. Image source: Wikimedia Commons.

In Kiryat Shmuel with our Israeli friends from Kiryat Haim. I am standing first on the line inside the fence.

Kibbutz Sarid in the Valley of Jezreel, late 1940s. Image source: Israel National Photo Collection.

# Kiryat Shmuel

The Jewish Agency's camp in Kiryat Shmuel was closed and fenced. It was guarded by Notrim – the Yishuv's Jewish police, supervised by the British. We went through the process of registration as a Youth Aliyah group and they told us that we would be on standby, waiting for an opening in one of the kibbutzim.

We had hoped that the Atlit camp would be the last fenced and guarded place for us. But in Kiryat Shmuel, we were still not allowed to get out of the camp. Under the terms of the Jewish Agency's agreement with the British, the immigrants had to remain confined to the camp until a sponsor assumed responsibility for their financial support.

As former prisoners in the Nazi camps, it was obvious that being locked up again was a painful thing for us. But in those times of confrontation with the British, the Yishuv and the Jewish Agency did not pay much attention to such considerations.

Our strongest wish was to be free of the fences and the wretched shacks and barracks that had been our "companions" all through the war. We badly wanted to be free, normal persons - to study, work and stop depending on others. We were full of vigor and wished to start a new life.

Time was against us. Youth Aliyah took care of children and teen-agers up to the age of eighteen. Any delay in our release could mean losing the right to benefit from the Youth Aliyah program. We would not be able to complete our education and professional training, which we saw as the best path to find a good place in society as a group and as individuals.

We complained to the Jewish Agency officials about the delay in the Kiryat Shmuel camp but to no avail. In the meantime, nobody from Mizra visited or contacted us. We knew that the severance was final. Fortunately, we had many visits from members of the Kiryat Haim branch of Hashomer Hatzair. They came every evening, sat on the other side of the fence, and we chatted and sang together. They were about our age, and in some cases our affinities led to romantic relations. Those were our first meetings with the youth of Eretz Israel – free, open, and spontaneous.

Of course, there were differences in mentality. We were less open, shy, and overwhelmed by their cheeky language, especially that of the girls. They probably overdid it to impress us. We spent many evenings together and I remember very well the atmosphere of freedom and homeliness. Some of them were later among the founders of Kibbutz Nachshon. One member of that group, Aharon Cohen, married my wife's best friend, Batya. Today we live within walking distance in the same city and we continue to be close friends.

Luckily for us, the stay in Kiryat Shmuel was not too long. We were notified that we would go to Kibbutz Sarid as a group entitled to Youth Aliyah benefits. They told us that Sarid was located near Mizra. We were not especially excited by that. We just acknowledged it with deliberate indifference. We were no longer interested in reuniting with the part of the group that had come first. It was the Hashomer Hatzair kibbutz organization that wanted to keep open the option of reuniting the group as possible founders of a new settlement in the future.

A woman and a man from Kibbutz Sarid, Frieda and David, came to the camp in a truck loaded with food, fruit and clothes. They introduced themselves as the kibbutz' teachers and guides for our group. We had a meeting in which they gave us details about kibbutz life in general and about the economic and social structure of Kibbutz Sarid in particular. They told us that our daily schedule would include four hours of study and four hours of work. We would be able to choose to work in any occupation that was available in the kibbutz. They also made a list of our collective and individual needs and requests, promising to do their best to fulfill them.

David and Frieda emphasized that Kibbutz Sarid was very keen on receiving our group and providing a warm home for us. They explained that we were their first group of young Holocaust survivors and that the people of the kibbutz did not want to fail. They advised us to be open and frank about our problems and reassured us that they would try to solve them to the best of their ability. Before leaving, they told us that they would finish the preparations and come back to take us to Sarid within the next couple of days.

Our future guides made a good impression on us. We were glad that we would be able to continue studying. We calmed down and cast aside our fears and suspicions. We had received proof that we would be taken care of.

Within the group, there had been arguments and debates about our collective future. There were two sectors in our group. One of them was the small core of activists, including me, who had grown up as members of the Hashomer Hatzair movement in Poland. We were very committed to the group, devoting a lot of our time and energy to nurture togetherness. The other sector included those who had joined later under various circumstances. Their identification with collectivist values was more superficial and they were less invested in the social life the group. These differences had been a source of conflicting attitudes and arguments. Usually the active core prevailed and we had managed to keep the group united.

# Free

By the end of January 1947 the much-expected day finally arrived. We left behind the fences, the guards, the barracks, and the oppressive atmosphere. We crossed the camp's gate singing, jolly and happy. We were finally free and on our way to Kibbutz Sarid.

With curiosity and amazement, we looked at every new thing on the sides of the road. We saw a country growing and blooming. The orange orchards impressed us a lot. As we approached Haifa, the landscape was very different to what we had expected. Instead of a desolate land, an endless desert with camels and sandstorms, we saw a big modern city, white houses, and blooming greeneries.

We stopped at a gas station for refueling and got a chance to walk around freely in the city. It was a wonderful feeling. Only someone who had been locked up for years could understand it. Our guides treated us to cones of ice cream and we continued towards the Valley of Jezreel. From far away we could see its beauty - the green open spaces and the black fertile soils ploughed and sown. There were tractors and people working in the fields. We had seen cultivated lands in Europe, but we had never seen Jewish farmers.

Approaching Sarid, the truck passed a grove of tall pine trees, turned to the right, and took a road lined by palm trees. When we crossed the kibbutz' gate the sight was overwhelming. It was a splendid farm with a big cowshed, hundreds of cows, a huge barn filled with hay, tractors and agricultural machinery, chimneys and towers. People were going around dressed in work clothes, happy, healthy and proud. It was a new world. The wonderful scene captured our hearts.

# PART V

# Sarid

Our reception in Kibbutz Sarid was extraordinary. In the evening, all the members of the kibbutz gathered in the dining hall for a festive dinner. There were performances and speeches. One of us thanked the kibbutz and presented a brief history of our group. From the first moment, we felt welcomed. The kibbutz members were not patronizing or distant. To the contrary, we felt that their doors were open to us and they wanted our friendship. Most of them had relatives who had perished in the Holocaust.

Our group, Geulim, was lucky to be assigned to Sarid. The founders of the kibbutz were educated people. Many of them were physicists, mathematicians, musicians, etc. They had given up the status and prestige of their professions in order to settle on the land, work in agriculture, and make the Zionist revolution a reality. Despite the age difference, they connected with us in an admirable way. The calm, serene atmosphere of the kibbutz had a big impact on us.

David, who spoke Polish quite well, was our teacher and mentor. Frieda, who had been born in Romania, spoke Yiddish. More than a guide, she was like a mother to all of us, individually and as a group. We loved and worshiped her. She was patient, good hearted, honest and firm. She gave us warmth and care, but knew how to keep us in line and make sure that we fulfilled our tasks.

David was a first rate teacher, very conscientious about his work. He was a man with wide horizons, knowledgeable in the humanities and sciences. At first, he tried to teach us in Polish. We rebelled, insisting that we wanted to study in Hebrew. We spent half of the day in class, willingly and happily. Thanks to our dedication, the curriculum was expanded in breath of subjects and depth. At the same time, we worked under the supervision of other members in the different economic activities of the kibbutz. We became close with many people and were friendly with everyone.

We had less interaction with the younger people of the kibbutz because most of the time they were away, studying in a boarding high school in Kibbutz Mishmar Haemek. We were very sorry about that.

I enjoyed every moment in Sarid - the freedom, the open-mindedness, the caring, the cornfields, the vineyards and the groves. We loved the atmosphere and the members of the kibbutz were our personality models. We wanted to be like them – healthy, strong and modest.

Among the kibbutz members were important national figures including Shlomo Rozen (later the minister of immigration absorption), Moshe Tzipor (editor of the newspaper Al Hamishmar), Amitay (another journalist), Natan Yonatan and his wife Tzfira (he was a poet and she a musician), and many others – all of them gifted and modest. They were friendly with everyone, behaving like ordinary folks. To this day I appreciate those dedicated, honest people who were content with little and helped others.

The year and a half that we spent in Sarid laid the foundation for our ability to build a new life in Israel. We shed the habits that we had acquired as prisoners in the Nazi camps. In behavior, clothing and style of speech we became like the Sabras (the Hebrew appellative for the youngsters born in Eretz Israel).

In addition to studying and working, we started military training with the Palmach. We learned to use light weapons and fulfill assignments such as patrols, ambushes and vigilance. In one of those trainings, we were discovered by a British patrol. We ran to a grove and managed to hide. We were lucky to get away.

One night I had an unpleasant incident. I had been assigned to a check post in a grove overlooking the fence. It was dark after midnight and I was very alert. We were on the threshold of the Independence War and the whole region was tense. Sarid was close to Nazareth, surrounded by Arab villages and Bedouin groups who had been stealing cows and sheep. Suddenly I sensed movement. I stopped breathing trying to concentrate. Was it a shrub stirred by the wind? Maybe a passing animal? I got tense, making an effort to adjust my eyes to the darkness.

After a few minutes I heard it again - a distinct rustle. I shouted the codeword. No response. I shouted again: "I am shooting!" After another warning, I loaded the rifle and fired a bullet. Only then I heard the clamor: "Do not shoot! We are checking the alertness of the guards!"

It was a miracle that I did not hurt them. I angrily asked why they had not responded to the codeword. They said that they wanted to put me to a real test. They congratulated me for passing the test but I was very upset by the fact that I could have killed someone.

When I finished my shift, my instructors talked with me about the incident. They told me that I had acted correctly and that the checking unit had been wrong in taking an uncalculated risk. All the same, I was very distressed. It took me time to recover from the anxiety caused by the incident.

Following the November 1947 decision of the United Nations to split Palestine into two states, the Arabs attacked the Jews and the Independence War began. We worked with the Kibbutz members digging ditches and trenches while we waited for our recruitment for full time service with the Palmach. We did not feel comfortable staying in the kibbutz while most people of our age were already fighting.

During the first months of 1948, as the British were preparing to leave, Jews and Arabs were maneuvering to take hold of their vacated military positions. Kibbutz Sarid was near the British airbase of Ramat David and the race was on about who would control the airfield. In April, the Iraqi army entered the Jezreel Valley and besieged Kibbutz Mishmar Haemek. We heard their cannons bombing the kibbutz. The Hagana succeeded in repelling the attack. According to knowledgeable people, it was an important strategic victory. The Iraqis withdrew and the situation improved in the entire Jezreel Valley.

In Sarid, however, the sense of relief was short-lived. We received the sad news that the brother of Raya, a member of our group, had been killed while escorting a supplies convoy to Kibbutz Yehiam in the Galilee. He had protected Raya throughout the Second World War with the partisans in the forests. For her, he had been everything, the only person in the world. We were heart broken by her grief.

Raya lost her brother just a few days before our recruitment. The tragedy was a warning of the dangers that we would face in the army. It also foreshadowed the cost of the approaching war.

# Mobilized

On May 14th 1948, the day in which the British Mandate over Palestine formally expired, the Yishuv proclaimed the independence of the State of Israel. A few days later, the Palmach mobilized our group for full service. They sent us to camp Yona near Beit Lid for training. It was a full military camp - closed, fenced, and with permission required for entering or leaving. There was no free time, simply because of the need to train additional fighting forces as quickly as possible.

There were no ranks or orders in the camp. Everything was done without ceremony, relying on mutual esteem and understanding. That was the fundamental attitude in the Palmach, and it worked well because everybody was highly motivated. In camp Yona there were no differences between the Sabras and us. We appreciated the extent to which our stay in Sarid had contributed to our adaptation. Most of us were able to keep up with the Israeli youth in all respects. There were, of course, some exceptions – a few of our group's members claimed that the Sabras were patronizing. I saw it as a matter of how much different individuals could deal with new, changing situations. Personally, I did not feel any patronizing.

The trainings were hard. We were told time and again that exertion was essential to improve our odds of winning the war and surviving. We understood it very well. Every day there was news about soldiers killed and wounded. The war was raging on several fronts. The Negev was besieged. Our forces were still trying to prevail in the Fallujah Pocket (nowadays Lachish region) and Beer Sheba. The police fort of Iraq-es-Suweidan (now Metzudat Yoav) near Kibbutz Negba was in the hands of the Egyptians. The post of Eilat (then called Umm Al-Rashrash) was still in the hands of the Jordanians. There were intense battles in the Galilee and the road to Jerusalem was blocked. We knew that we were going to join the force in the south, the Negev brigade commanded by Nahum Sarig from Kibbutz Beit Hashita.

During training, I had a serious leg injury and was taken to the Haemek hospital in Afula, not far from Sarid. My right leg was plastered for three weeks. On top of the pain, I felt bad that I would not be able to go with my group to the front. After two weeks I asked the doctors to open the plaster, claiming that I did not feel pain and that I could walk without help. When they opened it, I was truly scared. My leg had shrunk and was thin as a toothpick. The doctors explained that it was a common phenomenon - after a while, the leg would return to its normal shape.

I asked to be released from the hospital and go back to the camp. The doctors refused, saying that I had to rest for an additional two weeks and then get the necessary treatment for strengthening the leg. Frieda, our group's "mother," showed up at the hospital with goodies and treats. She told me that a car was waiting outside to take me to Sarid, where I would continue my treatment. Two days later, I heard that my group had finished their training in camp Yona and were about to be deployed to the front.

Our Sarid guides were going to visit the group before its departure from camp Yona. They agreed to take me with them. The moment I reached the camp I decided that I would not return to Sarid. I argued with the guides to convince them to let me stay with the group in camp Yona. It was against the doctors' orders and contrary to regular procedure. The guides demurred, but I insisted until they accepted my decision to stay.

By nature I am not an adventurer and I usually obey instructions, but the desire to be with my comrades at that critical moment overcame all other considerations. I just could not put up with staying behind while they went to the front.

I joined the group without reporting to the commanders that I was not fully recovered. We soon departed to the southern front. After a long drive, we arrived in the middle of the night to Kibbutz Negba, whose members had heroically repelled the Egyptians with last minute help from the Palmach.

Without any delay, we marched into the night escorted by a road-guide. As we approached the enemy lines we were instructed to slow down and maintain strict silence. From a distance of about 200 meters we saw the Iraq-es-Suweidan fort with all its fences, watchtowers and lights. The fort was still in the hands of the Egyptian army, which had mined the surrounding area.

The Egyptians fired flares that illuminated the battlefield as bright as daylight. Behind the fences, their dogs barked like maniacs. Our only choice was to advance crawling, connected with each other by codeword.

For hours we crawled on our bellies loaded with equipment and holding the rifles in our hands. Our progress was very slow and difficult. My leg hurt like hell. The only thing that kept me going was the drive to be with the rest of the group. In that extreme situation, I realized that I had been utterly irresponsible. If I failed, they would be forced to take care of me, which would cause delays and put at risk the whole operation.

I fought the pain and fear with all my strength. After several hours of crawling, we managed to circumvent the fort. Our commanders told us to stand up and start walking. My body was almost paralyzed and my senses were numb. I could not get up. Two of my mates helped me stand on my feet. I was dizzy, but the only alternative was to readjust to walking and endure the flares of pain from my leg. With the help of my friends, I managed to catch up with the others.

Behind enemy lines, we met with a force that had arrived before us. They held a fortified height that controlled a wide area. It was time to talk with the commander about my physical state. He understood my motives but he reproved me for not telling him before we started our mission. He said that we would deal with the problem later and sent me to the medical unit to take care of the leg and rest as much as possible.

The medical practitioner bound my leg with an elastic bandage and gave me tranquilizers. When the road-guide came by to ask how I was, he was shocked to see my shrunken leg grinded from the crawling. He scolded me for my reckless behavior and threatened to report me.

My guilty conscience depressed me. I was a burden on my mates. Fortunately, my friends were there for me, especially the medical practitioner. He told me to walk as much as possible and gave me massages. After several days, my muscles strengthened and my leg started to recover its shape. There was nobody happier than me.

I started functioning normally. I did guard duty and participated in ambush exercises. The commander appreciated my efforts and said that he would not report my blunder. We became friends.

The conditions at the post were difficult. The roads were blocked and there was no regular food supply. Drinking water was measured, hygiene conditions were bad, and everything was improvised and temporary. The hostile environment and the closeness of the

Egyptian lines sharpened our senses. Both sides had intelligence units exploring the area. We had to be permanently on the watch and avoid detection by the enemy. The success of the operation depended on the element of surprise. The Egyptians had to be kept in the dark about the presence of an Israeli force behind them.

During the next few nights our side succeeded in smuggling more forces behind the Egyptian lines. In the meantime, there were several failed attempts to take the Iraq-es-Suweidan fort.

One night we were eyewitnesses to a battle that took place not far from us. It was the famous conquest of the village Hulikat. Our forces used a flamethrower that made an enormous noise. The device had a big psychological impact, forcing the frightened villagers to run away. All the same, it was a hard and bitter battle. Many of our soldiers were killed or wounded.

Several days later we broke the deadlock, opening a land-mined road and making possible the arrival of troops to continue the war. After participating in the conquest of Beer Sheba, we returned to our post to secure the road and the occupied territory. Later we heard that the Negev brigade had taken other areas around Iraq-es-Suweidan, preparing the ground for the capture of the fort during Operation Shmone.

Following the seizure of the northern part of the Negev, we were sent back to an army camp near Beer Yaakov in central Israel. There, we took an advanced one-month course in communications. We learned to operate wireless radio, Morse alphabet, flags and heliograph signaling. The subject matter was knotty and the fieldwork required a lot of physical effort. Still, considering the conditions in the front, it was an enjoyable and refreshing break.

During the course we renewed our contact with Kibbutz Sarid. Our guides came to visit and brought us anything we needed. They made arrangements to allow our group's girls to join the communications course, which provided an opportunity to strengthen the social relations within the group.

Following the course, we were assigned to separate units of the brigade as signalers. The posting depended on the recommendations of the instructors. Some people were more successful than others in attaining the ability to decipher Morse and coded messages. In most cases, it was more a function of will and application than a matter of intelligence. Since I had put a lot of effort and had excelled in the course, I was posted as signaler of the brigade headquarters.

After conquering the police fort of Beit Jibrin, the brigade moved to secure that region. We settled in several positions in the area of Mount Hebron. We had to install a telephone line about fourteen kilometers long, stretching from the police fort, through the village of Kaukab Abu al-Hija, and to the village of Al-Dawayima (now Moshav Amatzya). Several members of our group, including a girl named Ruth and me, were part of the team.

When we reached the outskirts of Kaukab, Ruth shouted that she had seen someone among the buildings. Ruth had gained a lot of experience with the partisans in the Polish forests, so we knew that anything she said had to be taken seriously. We used our wireless to contact headquarters in the Beit Jibrin fort. They told us to carefully check the area and go on with the job if we found that it was clear. We entered the village carefully, walking beside the car with our guns ready for action. We combed the village but we did not see anything. We finished the task and returned to our base.

Later that afternoon a truck with supplies went to the Al-Dawayima post. When it approached Kaukab it was attacked by ambushed Arabs. Some of the soldiers were wounded and killed. After the incident, a check and search operation was conducted. The inquiry discovered that the Arabs had opened fire on the truck through openings in a stone fence. Ruth had been right – there was someone there. She was praised for her keen observation skills.

The region was very dangerous. Armed Arabs were roaming around hungry, homeless, and willing to take risks in order to get food. At one point, they even succeeded in breaking in and stealing supplies from our headquarters' food store.

We had another painful incident in the Beit Jibrin region. Three armed units were sent on foot on a scouting mission. There was wireless connection between the units and with headquarters. The scouts' commander, whose nickname was Penny, had reputation as a brave fighter. While scouting a dry riverbed, his unit ran into a grazing herd of sheep. The commander saw a shepherd watching the herd from the top of the mountain. He contacted headquarters and asked for instructions. I received his message on the wireless and informed the brigade commander. He instructed me to respond: "Leave the shepherd alone and go on with the task." The scouts' commander did not obey the order. He seized the herd and started leading it to the base. The shepherd requested help from the nearest Arab village on the other the side of the border. A big armed crowd came down, took back the herd and killed the eleven soldiers of the unit, including the commander. They not only shot them – they slaughtered them. The soldiers were cut into pieces and had to be brought back in sacks. One of them was a friend from Mizra who had survived the Nazi camps. Like me, he had lost his entire family. Now he had lost his life as a result of a serious case of disobedience that took a horrible toll in human lives. I do not know if that incident was ever investigated.

Rashness, exaggerated self-confidence, and scorn for the fighting ability of the enemy was a common phenomenon among young commanders. Perhaps it was a reflection of the tempers of the times.

The massacre shocked the regiment. Despite the grief, we had to recover quickly and go on with our operational activities. We continued our regular checks to make sure that we had an open telephone line. We often found that the Arabs made improvised connections with safety pins that enabled them to listen and pass on the information about our operations to their intelligence officers.

The Arabs of the Mount Hebron area were known for their religious fanaticism. During the British mandate, they had been very active in murder operations against the Jews. In 1929 the Jews of Hebron had been massacred. The survivors had to evacuate the town and the Arabs took all the Jewish property.

We were in control of the Beit Jibrin region but the war was far from over. They transferred us to the Bilu camp near Rehovot, in the central zone of Israel, for reorganization and advanced training.

The group was reunited and we felt better, but not for a long time. Part of the group, including me, was temporarily attached to the 7th Battalion of the Palmach for Operation Uvda, whose purpose was the conquest of Eilat. The operation was physically demanding because we had to drive and walk a long way in hostile desert conditions. The goal was to reach Umm Al-Rashrash, the Jordanian border post on the beach of the Red Sea. We completed the mission quickly, without enemy resistance. When we arrived, we found three small empty buildings and a cooking fire still burning in the yard – evidence that the Jordanian guards had just fled in a hurry.

The Umm Al-Rashrash post was conquered without Jordanian resistance on March 10th 1949. That operation established the southern borders of the State of Israel. It was a privilege to participate in it.

We prepared for a long stay in desert conditions. The first weeks were very difficult. The road was terribly inadequate and it took time until they were able to improve it for use by the trucks.

In the meantime, we were disconnected from the inhabited part of the country and without a regular supply of water and food. For three months we had to do with dry biscuits and preserved orange juice. I set up the wireless station in the highest place, then called Ras-el-Nakeb. From there, I handled communications with our regiment's headquarters in Hatzor. My station was the "nerve center" of the soldiers stationed in Eilat. It was always full of people, sending and receiving messages day and night.

Later on, the whole regiment, including the other members of our group, joined us in the Negev. The troops were stationed across the entire southern part of Israel in a series of posts from Beer Sheba to Eilat. The connection between members of our group was renewed through telegrams and messages between wireless stations.

Operation Uvda was the last campaign of the Independence War. The Palmach was dismantled and its troops were reabsorbed into the structure of the newly established Israel Defense Forces. Many fighters took offense. They thought that the disbanding of the Palmach was more a political decision than a military one. In any case, all the pioneer training groups that had been recruited were sent back to the kibbutzim. In fact, our group was discharged immediately after the last battle. After being merged with an Israeli group, the group spent time in Sarid and then in Kibbutz Dalya on Mount Carmel, waiting to be assigned the lands to establish a new independent kibbutz.

But not everyone was released - indispensable soldiers had to go on serving in the army. Unfortunately, I was one of the three members of the group who were not demobilized.

Soldiers of the Negev Brigade overlooking the fort of Iraq-es-Suweidan. Image source: Wikimedia Commons.

Palmach soldiers – my friends and me.

After conquering the fort of Beit Jibrin, we settled on several positions in the area of Mount Hebron.

The police fort of Beit Jibrin.

Operation Uvda: the Negev Brigade on the way to Umm Al-Rashrash. Image source: Palmach Museum.

Soldiers raising the Israeli flag in Eilat. Image source: Israel National Photo Collection.

# Separated from the group

I was troubled by the fact that I could not join my friends. We had been through a lot together and we had shared plans for our future. I tried to keep in touch as much as possible. The opportunities for visits were rare, short and hurried. During one of the visits to Dalya I met Dikla, who would become my dear wife and lifetime companion. Seeing her became another powerful reason to visit the group.

The separation and distance, however, began to affect my connection with the group. For one thing, there were changes in the group itself - other people had joined and new developments altered its social life and prospects.

My personal situation also changed. For the first time I was on my own and had to take care of my needs by myself. My self-confidence grew stronger and I met new people from different walks of life across the country. I began to think about the possibility of alternatives to living in the kibbutz.

That period was not easy for me. Since the choice of a different path was a matter of conscience, I debated with myself. In the midst of that, the central office of the Hashomer Hatzair kibbutz movement made a decision that would have important consequences. They assigned our group to Kibbutz Nahshonim, a young settlement near Rosh Haayin. Our group's dream to found a new kibbutz was erased in one stroke. Disappointment and anger led to a wave of desertions, especially among the new Israeli members of the group. They had homes and families in the country, and some of them wanted to continue studying.

I followed from a distance the debates that took place in the group. They focused on the prospects for the group's integration in Kibbutz Nahshonim. There were concerns about the founders' disposition to allow new members to participate equally in all the committees and lines of work. In the end, the group decided to accept the movement's decision and join Nahshonim.

I kept visiting them in Nahshonim. Dikla and I noticed a growing unhappiness among the group members. In private conversations, some of my closest friends told me that they wanted to leave or join another kibbutz because they did not have a good rapport with the founders. All of this confirmed my perception that the group was in crisis. Clearly, the decision to join an existing kibbutz had been a big mistake.

My first long visit to Nahshonim is a story worth telling. After three months of continuous army service, I had received leave for a week. I decided to visit Dikla and the other members of the group. Because of the lack of regular transportation, it took me two days to get from Eilat to Beer Sheba. After spending the night in a place arranged by the town's mayor, I finally arrived to the junction of Rosh Haayin on Friday evening. From there, it was about 10 kilometers to Nahshonim. It was already Shabbat and there was no bus service.

It was raining heavily and I did not have an umbrella or anything else to cover myself. I stood at the junction for an hour and a half waiting for a lift that never materialized. In the end, I began to walk. Two hours later, I reached the gate of the kibbutz wet to the bone. The gate was locked and I did not see any guards. I lifted the barbed wire and pushed myself to the other side of the fence.

I arrived tired, wet and hungry but happy. Dikla was surprised and very excited to see me. She dried my clothes and took care of everything. Later, I was told that I had taken a big risk walking from the junction to the kibbutz. We were close to the border and the army posts were on alert because of recent Arab infiltrations from the adjacent no-man land. I had been lucky that I had not been spotted and shot by our own soldiers or by the kibbutz guards when I crawled under the fence.

In those days, Kibbutz Nahshonim looked like a neglected army camp – just shacks on a hill without paths or roads. It was hard to go from one place to another because of the mud. There was an improvised dining shack where the members had their meals in three shifts. Water was brought once a week in a container. The men worked in the stone quarry in Migdal Tzedek and the women in a makeshift hospital in Rosh Haayin for the babies of new immigrant families from Yemen. Part of our group was still in Kibbutz Dalya and some of the Nahshonim members were still in their former location near Ramat Hasharon. The kibbutz was just in its earliest beginnings. On that visit, I put in several days of work laying road stones in the mud. I wanted to contribute my share, rather than being there just as a guest.

Not long after my visit, Dikla left the Kibbutz in order to continue her studies. She enrolled in the teachers' college at Givat Hashlosha. I was still in the army but we decided to get married. The wedding was on March 30, 1950. Dikla was eighteen and I was almost twenty-two. At that time, I was serving near Jerusalem, guarding the post of Ramat Rachel on the Jordanian border. In Israel's early days, telephones were a rare commodity, so Dikla and I kept in touch through letters and postcards.

I was still in the army but we decided to get married. The wedding was on March 30th 1950. Dikla was eighteen and I was almost twenty-two.

View of Kibbutz Nahshonim, 1950. Image source: Wikimedia Commons.

## Signs of life from my family

One day, Dikla's young cousin Benjamin heard on the radio that someone was looking for Yitzhak Weizman. He wrote a note with the details and sent it to Dikla.

It turned out that a woman called Tzipora Beckmeister was trying to find me through the radio program "Looking for Relatives." Dikla and I went to Tel Aviv to look for her. When we found her, she told us that she had come to Eretz Israel before the war. She had a cousin in Paris, Shlamek, who had asked her to look for me in Israel.

That was how I found out that Shlamek, my cousin from Zychlin, was alive and living in France. Some acquaintances had told him that they had seen me in one of the camps during the war and that he should check whether I had survived.

I was very happy to find that I had a relative in Israel – a distant relative but someone who was familiar with the past. Tzipora told me that Shlamek was the only survivor of his immediate family. I wrote to him and, five years after the end of the war, I finally received a sign of life from a close relative. We could not believe that we had found each other. Fortunately, Shlamek's first letter included details that confirmed it. He really was my cousin, the son of my mother's sister Rachel.

Since he was eleven years older than me, Shlamek had a better recollection of family details. I felt as if I had a newly born cousin, and he felt the same. From family visits, I remembered him as a high school student dressed in uniform, as was customary then in Poland. He remembered me as a small child sitting on his father's knees. We had different memories according to our relative ages at the beginning of the war.

Shlamek helped me find the relatives from my father's family who had immigrated to France before the war. I gave Shlamek the information I had about Aunt Anna, but I had forgotten that another brother of my father, Moshe Aharon, had also gone to France. Shlamek located both families in Paris. He told me that Uncle Moshe Aharon, who went by his French name Maurice, had arrived before Aunt Anna, at the age of thirteen. All of that had a strong emotional meaning - it connected me again to my roots.

Shlamek had spent most of war in Łódź ghetto with his family. The city of Łódź had already been an industrial center before the war. Following the occupation, the Germans annexed Łódź to the Reich and established a large ghetto where the Jews worked in workshops and factories. Of course, they were not paid – they just received food rations to stay alive. Shlamek's father, Yaakov Bol, died in the ghetto. His mother Rachel and his sister Fela were deported to extermination when the ghetto was liquidated towards the end of the war. Shlamek was sent to work in Germany and managed to survive.

In France, Aunt Anna and Uncle Moshe Aharon (Maurice) had spent the war hiding with their families in the countryside. They were lucky to find Gentiles who sheltered them in their farms in exchange for a lot of money. That was how they avoided deportation to the extermination camps. Still, Aunt Anna had lost a son. Bored in the village, he had gone to visit the city of Lyon, where the Germans were capturing hostages in retaliation for an attack of the French resistance. He ended up among those who were randomly seized in the streets. After the war, the family was told that all the hostages had been shot. Aunt Anna's daughter Harriet and her husband had stayed with them in the village and survived. They were a family of furriers and, after the war, they returned to Paris. They recovered their house and workshop and were able to reopen their business.

Aunt Anna was already an elderly woman, but when she learned that I had survived she came with her husband to visit me in Israel. I went to Haifa with my father-in-law Moshe to welcome her. When the ship arrived there were hundreds of people on the deck, but I recognized her immediately because of her resemblance to my father. We had arranged to accommodate them with Dikla's parents, but they preferred to stay with some friends from France who were living in Israel. I was annoyed and hurt. It was a pity that our first meeting was blemished by disappointment. Several days later, they came to visit us, bearing gifts that they had brought from France.

Later on, I wrote a letter to Aunt Anna about the way I had felt during her visit to Israel. Her answer was that I was too thin-skinned. It gave me food for thought. To be fair with my aunt, she corresponded with me for many years and they visited us again ten years later when we were living in Kibbutz Yad Mordechai. In 1976, Dikla and I visited them in Paris and all the members of Aunt Anna's family were wonderful hosts.

My aunt Anna and her husband Israel Glowinski.

Aunt Anna's daughter
Harriet with husband
Jacques Goldman.

My uncle Leon with his wife and her sister in Chile.

My uncle Maurice with his wife and daughter Paulette.

In the 1980s, another relative found me – Israel Magnes, cousin and close friend of my father. He told me about my father's political activism in Gombin and gave me some pictures. Israel Magnes and his wife Rivka had immigrated to Argentina before the war. There, they had three children who were members of Hashomer Hatzair. When their children came to Israel they decided to follow them and eventually settled in Rishon LeZion. Israel Magnes had been unaware that I had survived. Later on, when he began looking for me, he discovered that I also lived in Rishon LeZion. It was a remarkable coincidence and we were of course very happy about it.

# To independent life

Dikla concluded her studies and I finished at last my service in the army. At that time, we lived with Dikla's parents in Rishon LeZion. After much soul-searching, we decided to return to Kibbutz Nahshonim. We wrote to the kibbutz explaining our connection with the Geulim group. To our sorrow, we did not get any response. We then wrote to Kibbutz Yad Mordechai, where some of our friends were members. Without any problems we were admitted, first for a trial period and then as members.

Our first daughter, Ilil, was born in Yad Mordechai. Dikla was teaching and I was in charge of the plumbing branch. That branch dealt with the steam equipment of the communal kitchen and the industrial workshop, installation of water pumps and irrigation pipelines, and plumbing maintenance in all the buildings of the kibbutz.

It was a task of high responsibility that demanded long working hours. I had very little free time to devote to my family. Today, I still regret that I did not spend more time with my daughter. I was too young to understand the harm that could come from being addicted to work and neglecting the other important things in life.

After two and a half years, we left Yad Mordechai. The main reason was that Dikla and the kibbutz' committee had very different opinions about the educational needs of the youngsters who were under her responsibility. We went back to Rishon LeZion with a small child and penniless. However, we were not desperate. I started working in a big workshop in Tzrifin, an army base near Rishon LeZion. Shortly afterwards Dikla got a teaching job.

It was a time of housing shortages. We rented a one-room apartment. The bathroom was outside but at least it had running water. To say that the living conditions were inconvenient would be an understatement. We could not expect help from anyone, so we took a loan from Bank Hapoalim and started our independent life.

I worked in Tzrifin only for a short period. I liked the job and the managers were happy with me. I was more dedicated and skilled than most of the other workers. Some old-timers did not like it and started badgering me. Among other things, they intentionally sabotaged the equipment and machinery that I used in order to paint me as an inefficient worker.

I found a new job and resigned. The chief manager and the base commander tried to persuade me to stay, but my decision was final. I told them that I did not want to work with people who committed such acts against a workmate. It was obvious that my superiors knew about the hooliganism but they probably had reasons to ignore it.

My new job was in the cooperative factory Gavish. I started as an employee with special benefits. I was in charge of the maintenance of the factory, which produced glass products around the clock. There were three shifts and I had to make sure that the machinery functioned without interruptions. It was essential to operate the glass melting furnaces constantly. They had to be kept at a steady temperature of 1,500 degrees Celsius; otherwise, they would stop and cause economic losses. Officially, I worked eight hours a day with breakfast and lunch breaks. The reality was quite different. Very often, I had to stay longer, and I was frequently recalled from home because of some failure in the middle of the night, Sabbath and holidays included.

I was paid overtime for the extra work, but it was very hard for the family and myself. On top of that, the work conditions were tough – extreme heat, blaring noise, and suffocating dust. Most of the workers ended up with respiratory problems and partial or total deafness. Under today's regulations, such conditions would not be allowed, but in the 1950s, there was little awareness about workers' health.

As I became more involved in the cooperative, it was suggested that I should become a member. I liked the idea because I thought that it would increase my income. In the meantime, I had received a substantial sum of compensation money for forced labor in the German camps. Dikla sensibly thought that we had to use that money to buy our own apartment. Nevertheless, I was convinced that having a good income was more of a priority than buying an apartment. Dikla did not insist because she understood that it was important for me to be a member of the cooperative from a professional point of view. She also thought that, since it was my compensation money, I was entitled to decide what to do with it.

Panoramic view of Kibbutz Yad Mordechai.
Image source: Israel National Photo Collection.

With our first daughter, Ilil,
born in Yad Mordechai.

In Yad Mordechai, Dikla was teaching and I was
in charge of the plumbing branch.

Aunt Anna and her husband
visiting us in Yad Mordechai.

The family in 1963, with Dikla's parents Leah and
Moshe Yeffet, and our three children Ilil, Henat
and Hemy.

Enjoying our first vacation
trip to Europe in 1976.

I bought a membership share with the compensation money and part of my pension fund. After becoming a member, I was elected to the management. Only then did I get a clear view of the situation of the cooperative. It was in very bad shape, and the worse part of it was that we were late to do much about it. The cooperative had failed to bring in new technology and could not compete with the glass products that were imported into the country. The management had ignored the writing on the wall. The fact was that, rather than improving my economic situation, I lost a sum of money that was equivalent to the cost of an apartment. I could even lose my job, since there was a good chance that the cooperative would go bankrupt.

By then I was in my mid-thirties and we had had two more children - our second daughter Henat and our son Hemy. I had made a big mistake, but I did not give up. I had to learn the lesson and make the best of a bad bargain. I decided that studying and getting a professional certificate would be a better path to secure our family's future.

Thus, at the age of thirty-six I enrolled in the technological college Yad Singalovsky in Tel Aviv in order to get a teacher of technology certificate. In those days, Dikla was studying educational counseling at Bar Ilan University. We also decided to move out from our rented apartment. Since it was a rent-controlled property, the owner paid us some requital money that we used as a down payment towards a home. Now we owned our own apartment, but we had to pay the mortgage.

Returning to school after so many years was not easy. I worked in the cooperative during the day and attended classes four evenings a week. Concentrating in the studies took me a lot of effort. Dikla would wake me up very early in the morning to do the homework before I left to work. Sometimes I had to take pills for my headaches, which made me even sleepier and blurred my vision.

Yet, in spite of the difficulties, I enjoyed studying and received good marks. I did well in a situation in which most students were younger than me. After two years of college, I got the teacher of technology diploma. For the first time in my life, I could show a formal professional credential.

I finished my studies in 1967, before the Six-Day War. I was mobilized three weeks before the war started. My unit fought with the armored force that took over Um-Katef in the south. I returned home several days after the end of the war.

I applied to a number of high schools for a teacher's post. I chose Comprehensive School Alef in Ashdod. It was a new school where everything had to be done from scratch and the challenge was appealing to me. They gave me a free hand to organize the mechanics and craftsmanship departments.

While working in the school, I continued my evening studies in order to get a higher-level certificate. The higher qualification entitled me to a salary raise. By then, Dikla was studying mathematics at the University of Tel Aviv. Our first daughter Ilil studied mathematics and philosophy at the Hebrew University in Jerusalem and our second daughter Henat studied in a private high school in Tel Aviv. Our son Hemy was still in primary school, but later on he attended the same high school.

At the time, there was a shortage of teachers for technical subjects, especially in the south. Through self-directed learning and in-training studies, I improved my teaching to the point that, in the state's graduation tests, the results of my department's students were in most cases above average.

In 1983, I received a prize as the city's most outstanding teacher. The Minister of Education, the city mayor, the school principal and all the teachers attended the ceremony. It had been hard to earn that distinction. For many years, I had devoted myself to my work, day and night preparing lessons and correcting students' papers, and always worrying that I was not spending enough time with my family.

Most of the students in high school technological departments are low achievers who dislike school. They have to learn a trade and get a formal certificate. Sometimes they also have to pass general theoretical tests. They feel inferior because they did not qualify for the theoretical departments whose diplomas are required for entering universities. Frustrated and rebellious, they often turn their negative emotions against the teachers. As a result, teachers of technological departments face daily clashes with the class and with individual students. They must cover the curriculum, but at the same time, they have to change the attitudes of the students and help them understand that studying technological subjects is respectable and offers a good path towards a productive life.

A teacher's work never ends. There is constant interaction with the students. One has to prepare lessons, check papers, teach, test and evaluate. The students are persons with sensitivities and wishes that develop constantly. They are subject to many influences, from their family and friends to popular culture and the media. Teaching is grinding and tiring because none of these complexities can be ignored. With the passing of time, work became harder and harder for me.

Starting in 1976, we began to travel abroad during the summer vacations. Dikla insisted on it. She said, "There is a big world out there - it is time for us to see some of it and worry less about work for a change." We really enjoyed our trips. We visited many countries in Europe, Britain and North America. But we never went to Poland, Germany or Austria. I did not want to see the mass grave of my people.

At the age of sixty-three, I transitioned to half-time work and, after two years, I retired completely. I had worked as a teacher for twenty-seven years and I worried that perhaps I would miss it. As it turned out, I felt no regrets at all. My decision to stop working was right. I gave my best and enough was enough.

# Looking back

I have summed up memories and thoughts about my life, fulfilling the request of my children and grandchildren to tell them about my experiences during the Second World War.

I had never given details to them about what happened to my family and me during the Holocaust. I did not want them to feel personally connected with that terrible tragedy.

Over the last few years, I have been aware that my children want to know about the past. Now they are adults who can understand and ask the right questions, as much as it is possible for those who were not there. They are university graduates who can confront and meditate about the complex causes of the disaster that befell the Jewish people. I feel that I can talk with them as I have always talked with my wife Dikla, who is interested and knowledgeable in historical matters.

My grandchildren are also asking questions about their family roots. My grandson Dan, the oldest of the four sons of my daughter Ilil, was the first to show interest. His next brother Miki soon followed him. In most Israeli schools, students do a family roots research project in preparation for their Bar or Bat Mitzvah, so they asked me about my story and wrote about it in their papers. Mentally, the fact that my children and grandchildren wanted to know helped me a lot. It made it easier for me to open up.

Although fifty years have passed, I cannot forget and I cannot forgive, especially now that the Nazis in Germany are raising their heads again. It is impossible to stay indifferent and not to want to remind the world what the Nazi ideology did. Recently, the heirs of the owners of the company Topf und Sohne, which built the gas chambers and crematoriums in Auschwitz and other camps, showed no compunction in trying to reclaim the company property confiscated by East Germany. It seems that the insensitivity of the Germans has not changed. In fact, for more than a decade after the war, the nationalized company kept building crematoriums using the same patent approved by the Nazis.

Fifty years have passed. Most of the Germans who were then alive have already died or are old. Today's Germans are their children and grandchildren. However, our account with Germany is not yet settled. The Jewish "genetic code" remembers. We cannot forget the gas chambers, the crematoriums, and the cruelties and humiliations that we suffered as Jews and as human beings.

Fifty years have passed and yet the Germans are for me, and for many others like me, a hated nation. Can the "genetic codes" that garner all the anxieties and hatreds of the past ever change? Will the deeply rooted Christian belief about "Jewish treachery" ever fade away? Is it possible to change the perceptions that lead many Holocaust survivors to believe that "all the Gentiles are against us" and should not be trusted?

Will we ever be able to forget and forgive? Is it possible to settle the account when we are dealing with things that are so painful? Does the passing of time heal or does it only blur and postpone our thoughts?

The answers to these questions are relevant for our personal fate and for the future of Israel, the country that should be open and safe for all Jews wherever they are.

I was born and lived in an interesting, stormy and ghastly era. I was fortunate to survive the Holocaust. I am not a hero and I never wanted to be a hero. I only wanted to go on living. I saw the establishment of the State of Israel and fought in most of its wars. My life in Israel was not easy but I made an honest living for my family and myself, together with my wife Dikla who has not yet retired. I have lived as a free, proud person without ignoring the past and the experiences and events that left deep marks in my whole being. Whether or not I succeeded is for my family and friends to judge. As for me, I know that I did not go "like cattle to the slaughter." I fought a war of survival under horrendous conditions and prevailed.

# POSTCRIPTS

# 1997

On May 5, 1997, Israel observed the annual Memorial Day for the Martyrs and Heroes of the Shoah. Shortly after arriving home from a school where I had lectured about the Holocaust the telephone rang. The caller was a woman who identified herself as Ada Holtzman. In an apologetic tone, she said, "For a long time I hesitated to call you, but today is Memorial Day and I decided to call."

When I heard the name Holtzman, I immediately remembered Meir Holtzman, one of our guides in the Gombin branch of the youth movement Hashomer Hatzair. I asked her if she was his daughter and she confirmed it. Of course, the excitement was mutual. Ada told me that Meir was still around and was living in Kibbutz Ramat Hashofet since marrying again after the death of his first wife. Before that, he had had been a member of Kibbutz Evron, where he and his first wife Rivka had arrived just three months before the outbreak of the Second World War. Ada's mother Rivka was also a Gombiner from the Gostynski family, which was distantly related to my family.

Ada is a walking encyclopedia about the Jews of Gombin. As part of her research, she has been working in archives, writing, traveling, taking pictures, and collecting testimonies from Gombiners who are still alive. Ada was born in Kibbutz Evron and she has never lived in the Diaspora. Her parents were not Holocaust survivors, but they lost their families during the war.

For Ada Holtzman, preserving the memory of the Jews of Gombin is a lifetime job. She has visited the town on several occasions and is involved in the effort to restore the destroyed Jewish cemetery of Gombin. Ada told me over the phone that she had found my testimony in the archives of Yad Vashem and, a few days later, she sent me copies of survivor testimonies and various texts about other Gombiners who resettled in America and Israel before and after the war. Through these materials, I learned about the fate of some of the people I knew as a child in Gombin.

I found out that Dzunia Wolfowicz survived. She and her sister got false papers and spent the war in Warsaw passing as Poles. I remember Dzunia well. She had light hair and skin and spoke fluent Polish without an accent. We sat together on the same bench in primary school. Now her name is Ada Rakocz, she has seven grandchildren and lives in Israel in the city of Hedera.

Among the stories of families, I also recognized the name of a childhood friend, my neighbor Hershek Shvartz. Hershek had been there on the night that they took us to the Firemen's Hall for selection and transport to the labor camps. I did not see him because the hall was crowded with hundreds of men. They sent him home because he was too young. That determined his fate. Weeks later, the Germans dispatched him to extermination in Chelmno with his family and all the other Jews of the town.

Compared to the other families of Gombin, the Shvartz family is an exceptional case because almost all the brothers (Hershek's uncles) survived. I remember that just before the war one of Hershek's uncles immigrated to Panama with his wife and two young sons. Welvek, the older of the two children, was about my age and a good friend of mine. Ada told me that later he moved to the United States and gave me his address.

Through Ada Holtzman, I also got information about Mendel Wrobel, Zalman Tatarka and Lajzer Bocian – the three Gombiners who had been liberated with me. Lajzer, the youngest of them, has already passed away. He had two daughters, one of his own and the other adopted.

Ada gave me the address of Mendel Wrobel. I wrote to him and he immediately responded. We had a phone conversation and he was so emotional that he almost cried. He promised that he would put me in touch with Zalman Tatarka.

I also heard from Ada about the three Frenkel brothers - Shmuel, Chaim and Yankl. We were together in the Konin labor camp but from there the Germans deported us to different locations. Like me, they survived several camps including Auschwitz and Dachau. Later on, I met Chaim and Yankl in Italy. They were about to leave to Eretz Israel when they heard that Shmuel, the oldest brother, was alive in Germany. They went to Germany to look for their lost brother and found him. From there, the three brothers immigrated together to America, where they live today with their families.

This year, I attended a memorial service for the Gombiners who perished in the Holocaust and in Israel's wars. The ceremony took place at the Gombin House in Tel Aviv. I was amazed to hear that

Avraham Najdorf's daughter has been living in the country since 1932. She came with a delegation to the First Maccabiah Games in Tel Aviv and did not return to Poland. Her name now is Dora Makow and she lives in Haifa. She is an intellectual, a graduate of the Languages department of Warsaw University, still lucid her late eighties. In the chapter on the Konin camp, I wrote about the heroic deed of her father, her brother, and her brother-in-law. When I talked with Dora over the phone, I told her that she should be proud to be the daughter of a heroic Jewish family. I look forward to meeting her in person and tell her the whole story.

# 2003

My two daughters, Ilil and Henat, have visited Poland with their high school students. Four of my eight grandchildren have also been there: Henat's oldest daughter Tom, and three of Ilil's four sons - Dan, Miki and Shay. Those visits are part of the curriculum of Israel's high schools. It was a pity that Gombin was not included in their itineraries. My other four grandchildren are still too young, but they will also go to Poland as part of their high school education. Like all my older grandchildren, two of them have already written papers on their family roots as part of their Bar or Bat Mitzvah preparation in school.

When they were in Auschwitz with their school program, Tom and Shay read aloud some paragraphs from my memoirs. Their classmates listened attentively. Shay wrote a short journey diary in which he expressed his thoughts and emotions.

My son Hemy, a lawyer, has not been to Poland yet. On several occasions, he has tried to persuade me to go with him and visit Gombin. Every time I have refused, telling him that he will have the opportunity of accompanying his children as an escort parent when they go there with their school program. I remain faithful to my oath – I will never return to Poland. On the other hand, I appreciate that my children and grandchildren can go there, see the places, and meditate about the fate of the Jews during the Second World War.

In the last few years, I have been among the lecturers sent by Yad Vashem to talk with high school students and with young men and women serving in the army. In the meetings, the participants show a strong interest in learning more about the Holocaust, and it gives me comfort that I can make a small contribution to their knowledge about that immense tragedy. Hopefully, that knowledge will inspire them to reflect about the historical circumstances in which Israel was born and about the importance of having a Jewish state to make sure that a Holocaust cannot happen again.

Our eight grandchildren on my 75th birthday, 2003. From right to left: Dan Burde, Rotem Weizman, Noam Burde, Tom Landsberg, Michael (Miki) Burde, Shay Burde, Sefi Landsberg, Amir Weizman.

Celebrating my 80th birthday with our extended family in 2008.

With Dikla, my dear wife and lifetime companion.

www.ingramcontent.com/pod-product-compliance
Lightning Source LLC
Chambersburg PA
CBHW070441100426
42812CB00004B/1180